GOING BY THE BOOK

GOING BY THE BOOK

*The Role of Popular Classroom
Chronicles in the Professional
Development of Teachers*

Jane Isenberg

BERGIN & GARVEY
Westport, Connecticut • London

Library of Congress Cataloging-in-Publication Data

Isenberg, Jane.
Going by the book : the role of popular classroom chronicles in
the professional development of teachers / Jane Isenberg.
p.   cm.
Includes bibliographical references (p.   ) and index.
ISBN 0–89789–386–7 (alk. paper)—ISBN 0–89789–396–4 (pbk.)
1. Teachers—United States. 2. Teachers—Training of—United
States. 3. Education in literature.   I. Title.
LB1775.2.I84   1994
371.1′00973—dc20   93–43732

British Library Cataloguing in Publication Data is available.

Library of Congress Catalog Card Number: 93–43732
ISBN: 0–89789–386–7
     0–89789–396–4 (pbk.)

First published in 1994

Bergin & Garvey, 88 Post Road West, Westport, CT 06881
An imprint of Greenwood Publishing Group, Inc.

Printed in the United States of America

The paper used in this book complies with the
Permanent Paper Standard issued by the National
Information Standards Organization (Z39.48–1984).

10 9 8 7 6 5 4 3 2 1

Copyright Acknowledgments

In memory of

Marian and Hymen Siegendorf

Donald W. Isenberg

Jessie Benson

Contents

Preface

In the very act of writing this book, which is, in part, a rather elaborate thank-you note to the teacher-authors who have sustained me in the classroom, I have incurred yet another debt. So these few lines are also a thank-you note, simpler and shorter but no less heartfelt. This note is to the people who have sustained me at the word processor: Debbie Calahan, Joe Colicchio, Emily Dominguez, Margot Ely, Lynn Flint, Elaine Foster, Marge and Bill Graham, Barbara Grenquist, Amanda Gulla, Janis Isenberg, Liz Leiba, Corinne Levin, Lisa Lipkin, Liliane MacPherson, John Mayher, Taleasia McCants, Sharon Meyers, Michelle Nuding, Dennis Parsons, Henry Perkinson, Narcisa Polonio, Gordon Pradl, Ted Rabb, Joan and Joe Rafter, Jim Sacks, Sharon Shelton, Dinah Stevenson, Ruth Tait, Joe Todaro, Barry Tomkins, Ellen Turner, Mark Walker, and those at Hudson County Community College who awarded me a sabbatical leave during which to complete the book.

In addition, I belong to a writing group with Susan Babinski, Pat Juell, and Rebecca Mlynarczyk; this manuscript has benefited enormously from their informed and tactful counsel, as have I from their gift of sisterhood.

Rachel and Daniel Isenberg came of age while I was at the computer; Rachel, my Seattle-based muse, cheered me on by phone while Daniel served the more immediate function of critic, orderer of take-out food, and strummer of background blues. Phil Tompkins proofread the text at every stage, patiently walked me through innumerable word-processing crises, and kept me supplied with chocolate right through each deadline.

Introduction

What matters is that lives do not serve as models; only stories do that. And it is a hard thing to make up stories to live by. We can only retell and live by the stories we have read or heard. We live our lives through texts. They may be read, or chanted, or experienced electronically, or come to us like the murmurings of our mothers, telling us what conventions demand. Whatever their form or medium, these stories have formed us all; they are what we must use to make new fictions, new narratives.

Carolyn G. Heilbrun
Writing a Woman's Life

Inevitably, my efforts to navigate the daunting passage that is midlife have moved me to reflect at length on my thirty-year journey as an urban English teacher. When I began that journey in 1962, in room A301 at Smithfield High School in New Haven, Connecticut, I felt much like Alice after she stumbles into the rabbit hole. Just as Alice alternates between being too big to squeeze through the garden gate and too small to reach the key on the table, I did not fit in at Smithfield. Luckily, a caterpillar tells Alice how to change her size at will, facilitating her trip through the subterranean maze of Wonderland. It was

Sylvia Ashton-Warner, Bel Kaufman, E. R. Braithwaite,
John Holt, and Herbert Kohl who taught me how to
survive and teach in the urban classroom.

When, during the course of my recent musings, these
teacher-authors reappeared in my consciousness, I recalled
how they had validated my affection for many of my
students, as well as my horror at the biases and misan-
thropy of some of my colleagues; how they had shared
their mistakes and triumphs in the classroom with me, thus
helping me to recognize and acknowledge my own; how
they had made me cry over the implacability of "the
system," while at the same time showing me how to
manipulate its constraints; and how they had taken me
with them on their forays across cultural boundaries.

I wondered what a reunion with these early mentors
would be like. How would they fit in with my current
constructs? Would they be like my first college boyfriend,
sweet but no longer very interesting? Or would they still
loom as large, pedagogical greats who have made original
and lasting contributions to educational thought and
practice? Indeed, rereading the stories of these teacher-
writers proved to be so rewarding that I have made their
narratives my focus in this book.

Taking the reader with me through the looking glass of
memory to share my reflections on a long-ago time in a
faraway place poses certain challenges to us both. These
were made very clear to me recently when the director of
the Writing Center at Hudson County Community College,
where I have been teaching English since 1979, asked me
to deliver a talk to the center's tutorial staff on the book
I was writing. Some of the tutors were former students of
mine in English and speech classes. Moreover, I was
excited at the prospect of talking with people who, as
tutors, were already teaching, and who might someday
teach in other settings.

I prepared copies of an early draft of "The First Hundred Years," a section of chapter 1, to read with them. At

the workshop itself, we read aloud from the draft, and then I asked for responses. One woman queried: "Are you serious? Did that really happen?" This was easy to answer, since the tutors knew and trusted me: Yes, it really happened. Another question was: "What kind of school was that? Was it some kind of special school?" This was also easy to answer by referring to our current shared context. Hudson County Community College is special only in its specific urban setting, but nonetheless, it is very hard to explain to outsiders, and even some insiders.

But several tutors also wanted to know, "If you were so unhappy, why didn't you leave teaching and do something else?" In 1993 they asked this question of the fifty-two-year-old career teacher sitting comfortably among them, a familiar mentor who had helped several of them learn to speak in public, write for college, appreciate literature, use a word processor, and prepare for job interviews, and who had, in fact, recommended a few of them for the very tutoring positions they now held. They clearly had trouble imagining me as a terrified twenty-two-year-old girl who could not type fast enough to be a secretary. Like Bill Clinton during his presidential campaign, I found myself trying to explain to them what life was like just prior to the time when the civil rights, women's rights, and antiwar movements changed our laws and raised our consciousness.

To contextualize for readers the impact of the teacher-authors on me as a neophyte, in chapter 1 I briefly reflect on my own experiences as a high school student in the class of 1958 and on the preparation for teaching I received in college. Here and throughout the story, the names of all people and high schools I mention are fictitious; the colleges and most towns, however, are real. Next, I explicate the educational theories that dictated practice at Smithfield and describe the curriculum and institutional culture that greeted me there. My own

background and the educational assumptions and sociopo-
litical forces at Smithfield coalesce in the account of my
first year of teaching, which concludes this chapter.

By sharing how I experienced *Teacher, Up the Down
Staircase, To Sir, with Love, How Children Fail,* and *36
Children* in the early years of my career, I demonstrate the
enormous importance of popular teaching narratives such
as these in the professional development of educators. In
fact, it is by making a case study of myself and my experience as a preservice and developing teacher that I drama-
tize the crucial role that teaching narratives can play in
one's professional coming-of-age. In separate chapters I
consider each of the five teaching narratives that I encountered during the first seven years that I taught, recalling
my early responses to the books as well as noting my
recent reactions to them.

It is significant that *Going by the Book* is, in places,
itself a teaching narrative, a type of literature that is often
marginalized by literary critics, who claim it is merely
"popular," and educational theorists, who dismiss it as
merely "pragmatic." By reflecting on how particular
teaching narratives informed my own early practice, and
continue to inform it thirty years later, I illuminate a
frequently neglected source of professional wisdom.
However, it is important for my readers to understand that
I do not claim to have simply read the narratives and then
magically metamorphosed into a highly successful and
competent teacher. Rather, through my reading, I gained
insight into my own background, the cultures of different
schools, and the classroom work of others. Even more
important, perhaps, I tempered my isolation by acquiring
mentors to sustain me as I struggled, first to hang on and
hang in, and later to recognize and record my own story in
this book. Like most teaching narratives, mine is an
account of survival and gradual growth, and not, regrettably, a fairy tale of instant transformation and triumph.

While I focus on only those teaching narratives that I

actually read as a new teacher, there are countless others available to the curious reader. These works are a pervasive form of teacher lore and, as such, they are worthy of inclusion in the curricula of institutions devoted to teacher education. Therefore, in the study's final, and synthesizing, chapter, I establish the teaching narrative as like the slave narrative, another previously marginalized literary form that has only recently been recognized by literary critics and historians as fundamental to any serious consideration of American literature and history. The fact that the similarity between teaching narratives and slave narratives extends beyond their marginalized status is important in enabling my readers to comprehend both the socially constructed nature of marginalization and the particular structure and style of teaching narratives.

Equipped with the example of how I used teaching narratives at different stages of my own career, my readers will be prepared to understand the debate between those who demean research by classroom teachers and those who argue instead that the writings of classroom teachers are invaluable sources of insight and experience. Furthermore, in the review of this debate, the past, present, and potential value of teacher-narrators as generators of educational theory and witnesses to the idiosyncratic and complex nature of schooling becomes clear.

Finally, having argued for the legitimacy and utility of teaching narratives, I suggest some of the many ways in which teacher-educators can use them in their work with aspiring and midcareer educators alike. It is often the teacher-educator who acquaints neophytes with the literature of our profession and facilitates their interpretation and use of it. Likewise, it is frequently the teacher-educator who guides the reading of seasoned teachers, helping them interpret the same literature in light of their own experiences, knowledge, and wisdom.

Although I address directly the role of teacher-educators in guiding their students' exploration of professional literature, in the following story of my own encounters with teaching narratives, as well as my explication of their style and structure, I also hope to contribute to the validation of the voices and experiences of classroom teachers at all stages of our professional lives.

GOING BY THE BOOK

1

Stranger in a Strange Land

PACKING FOR THE TRIP

Actually, the world of Smithfield High, which I had entered in 1962, only became fully comprehensible to me more than twenty-five years later, when I began to investigate the history of secondary English education in the United States in preparation for this book. Doing this research was a little like looking at a map and discovering that a place I know well is not situated quite where I had thought it was. So as to orient the reader, I shall lay out some of my discoveries, charting the terrain I traveled, as I recreate the first leg of my teaching journey.

One reason for my discomfort in my new role was that much of what then I knew of English curriculum and pedagogy was limited to the futile efforts of my own high school teachers. These had been an assortment of mean-spirited, elderly women employed by Jersey High School between 1954 and 1958 to convince me of the merits of reading about boys who had to shoot their pets, miserly old Englishmen, Roman emperors so boring that they were killed by their close friends, and American men whose idea of fun was to write notes to themselves about the advantages of living near ponds in rural Massachusetts. I was supposed to appreciate these books and write about them ad nauseam, and I was not allowed to write or talk about anything else. I was also expected to do the grammar exercises in *Warriner's English Handbook* and memorize the definitions of countless vocabulary words. Moreover, the entire tedious drill was supposed to help me to get into college.

The dreaded College Board Exams proved, in fact, to be more interesting than my high school English classes, and so, much to the amazement of my teachers, I was accepted into college. Here I encountered the New Critics, who came in both genders. They stressed the formal and relational aspects of literary works which, it seemed to me, they wanted us to scrutinize in search of fairly abstract meanings rather than to simply read for pleasure and information. However, two out of the seven or so scholars with whom I studied during my Vassar career did have a sense of humor. Although as a high school student I had resisted the curriculum imposed by the Jersey High English faculty, as a college student I bought into that imposed by the New Critics. The illusion of choice created by registration, the freedom to smoke, eat, and sip coffee in class, the discovery that I was good at dissecting the great books in our professor-centered discussions—all this was heady stuff.

I have always loved to read. Also, I wanted very much to be cultured. It never once occurred to me that cultured meant Western-cultured, and that there were other worlds and other cultures that were excluded from Vassar's English curriculum at that time. The fact that my professors labeled my writing unscholarly and that I did not stay awake nights anguishing over the relative merits of form over content in "Kubla Khan" seemed unimportant. After all, my real goal at Vassar was to get married, and indeed, by the end of my junior year I was engaged. Rather than ending with me getting married and living happily ever after, my script, like those of many fiancées of future graduate students, stipulated that I get married and teach.

But before I could officially set out on my odyssey, I needed a passport in the form of certification. During the summers following my junior and senior years at Vassar, I took courses that included Human Development and Behavior I and II, as well as Methods and Materials in the Teaching of English, and Philosophy of Education at Montclair State Teachers College. I memorized the material required to pass these courses. Scheduling summer work around them and arranging transportation to Montclair made my summer studies enormously inconvenient; in addition, both courses were dull, but I was in love and no sacrifice was too great.

During my senior year I had to drop a contemporary poetry course and replace it with student teaching, which consisted of weekly forays of an hour or two into area junior high school classrooms: a suburban seventh grade in the fall, and a Poughkeepsie, New York, eighth grade just off campus in the spring. Although both master teachers were extremely nice to me, they taught in the familiar manner of my high school teachers, and I did not want to emulate them.

However, student teaching included participation in a seminar taught by Mrs. Goodwin, a kind, elderly woman who was highly regarded by Vassar's legions of Early Childhood Studies majors as a benevolent guru of progressive education. Perhaps for this reason, English majors, who tend to be a masochistic and elitist lot, disparaged her course as an easy "gut." But Mrs. Goodwin's seminar was memorable in spite of the fact that I knew nothing of progressive education and resented having to abandon my exploration of contemporary poetry. All we did was chat about our student teaching experiences. However, to this very day I can conjure up the image of elfin, bespectacled Mrs. Goodwin listening seriously and patiently to our sagas of student teaching and repeating softly, "You must remember, there is no such thing as a bad child." And while I did not understand her seemingly simple statement at the time, it lodged itself in my mind, echoing like a mantra through the ensuing decades.

Thus, bearing my certification and my diploma, as well as all the other baggage that nice Jewish girls routinely lugged around with them in 1962, I began the journey that has been my teaching career. Thanks to my highly touted Vassar education, I thought I was ready and, along with a battery of other Yale wives, I saw myself bringing the word to New Haven's teenage population.

TRANSMISSIONLAND

As Henry Perkinson explains in *Learning from Our Mistakes: A Reinterpretation of Twentieth Century Educational Theory*, early twentieth-century educators derived their pedagogy from the philosophy of John Locke, who said children were like "balls of wax that may be molded to the schoolmaster's wishes" (1984, p. 11). It was the responsibility of the teacher to transmit to the young, through rules, lectures, and dictums, the teacher's own knowledge and experience of the world. And, as John Mayher details in *Uncommon Sense: Theoretical Practice in Language Education*, there are other, similar metaphors for what he aptly describes as the "commonsense" learner and learning process.

These include the learner as empty vessel to be filled with the content of education, the learner as maze runner who needs to master the basics of complex processes by learning them separately and in appropriate sequence, the learner as sponge who absorbs information and squeezes it back out when appropriate, and the learner who practices through drills to develop good habits and avoid bad ones. (1990, p. 50)

Mayher points out that in all these metaphors, the

learner responds to stimuli, or ingests "undigested information," which he or she must soon regurgitate on a test. Since it is the teacher who is responsible for determining the knowledge to be transmitted and when and how the transmission is to take place, as well as how the effectiveness of the transmission is to be measured, it is no wonder that classroom teachers, and especially inexperienced ones, often feel overwhelmed with responsibility and inadequacy. It is no wonder that, as Mayher goes on to say, they spend long hours trying to devise successful techniques for molding the balls of wax, filling the vessels, immersing the sponges, and planning the skill drills, leaving very little time or energy for framing such questions as: "Is this how people really develop as readers? As writers? As thinkers?" Similarly, it is no wonder that students like the one I had been in Jersey High School or the ones I taught in room A301 at Smithfield High are less than enthusiastic about reading and writing in school.

Larry Cuban uses the metaphor of the school as factory, where learners are sorted into "niches" and teachers "distribute" the dominant cultural knowledge to the next generation. He concludes that "those teaching practices that seek obedience, uniformity, productivity, and other traits required for minimum participation in bureaucratic and industrial organizations, are viewed as both necessary and worthwhile" (1984, p. 240). In high schools, teaching practices tend to foster "competitiveness and productivity," both of which are "behaviors consistent with the requirements of the larger society" (1984, p. 241). Furthermore, Cuban claims that this capacity of the secondary school to mirror the values of our industrialized, socially stratified, and capitalist nation is largely responsible for the stability of classroom practice in this century.

In *Bitter Milk: Women and Teaching*, Madeleine Grumet looks at the impact of industrialization on education through the lens of gender, thus illuminating a more complex and inclusive perspective. She traces, among other things, the feminization of teaching in the context of the preoedipal responses of males and females as their fathers left the farm for the factory, forgoing the privacy of home and family for the public world of work. According to Grumet, who here cites Nancy Chodorow, this paternal exodus left children of both sexes "matrisexual" (1988, p. 47). Thus boys made the shift of identification from mother to father mandated by the oedipal crisis with more than usual unconscious regret and, conversely, girls, cooped up at home with their mothers, eagerly, but also unconsciously, sought paternal identification. Grumet suspects that it is in reaction to this abrupt schism in family life that, as adults, "male educators invited women into the schools expecting to reclaim their mothers, and the women accepted the invitation so that they might identify with their fathers. Female teachers complied with the rationalization and bureaucratization that pervaded the common schools as the industrial culture saturated the urban areas" (1988, p. 55).

Indeed, Cuban notes that even during its heyday in the early part of the century, the progressive movement in education, with its student-centered pedagogy, student-planned curriculum, small-group work, and flexible use of time and space, had much less impact on high schools than on elementary schools. Clearly, the English departments of neither Jersey High nor Smithfield High had succumbed to the lure of progressivism for long, if at all. For them, Dewey was only the name of the decimal system in the library. Cuban does offer several explanations for the relative imperviousness of the high schools to the charms of progressive teaching: more administrative support for progressive changes at the elementary level, "structural differences in content studied [and] instructional time spent with students, and differences in expectations between the lower and upper grades" (1984, p. 65). I would add that the greater number of men in secondary school teaching also made the high schools less hospitable to the spread of progressive pedagogy. The circular seating, small group work, and collaborative, nurturing, student-centered pedagogy of progressivism were not familiar to most men who were trained in and for authoritarian, hierarchical, and competitive settings such as traditional schools, gymnasiums, military barracks, and corporations.

To contrast it with progressivism, Cuban juxtaposes the transmission mode of teaching, which he captions as teacher-centered. He characterizes a teacher-centered classroom in this way:

Teacher talk exceeds student talk during instruction.
Instruction occurs frequently with the whole class; small group or individual instruction occurs less frequently.
Use of class time is determined by the teacher.
The classroom is usually arranged into rows of desks or chairs facing a blackboard with a teacher's desk nearby. (1984, p. 3)

Such was room A301 at Smithfield. Eileen Nolan, head of Smithfield's English Department, clearly believed that it was "possible to determine in advance not only what [students] need to learn but also the optimum sequence and means through which they should learn it" (Mayher, 1990, p. 57). She insisted that all nontenured English teachers submit weekly lesson plans on Monday mornings, which she ruthlessly edited.

Furthermore, Miss Nolan believed that quiet classrooms in which students worked individually to come up with the right answers to the assigned grammar, vocabulary, or study questions were the hallmark of an effective teacher. She encouraged me to preside over what Mayher and Rita Brause call "oral workbook" discussions (Mayher, 1990, p. 65), in which the teacher poses questions to the group and students vie to come up with correct but brief replies. Like the commonsense teacher that Mayher describes, Miss Nolan was opposed to students talking together at all. She often admonished me against smiling at my students, so firmly did she believe that their restlessness and boredom were somehow attributable to my facial expressions rather than our activities. I recalled her admonition recently when I read *Don't Smile until Christmas: Accounts of the First Year of Teaching*, edited by Kevin Ryan (1970). I was also reminded of Miss Nolan when I read *The Last Little Citadel* in which Robert L. Hampel discusses the political, social, and pedagogical conservatism of secondary school teachers in the early 1960s (1986, p. 86).

CULTURE: CONTROL AND CURRICULUM

But I do not mean to trivialize Miss Nolan's need for control. My colleagues and I worried about it all the time, understandably. Some students, who were not very interested in the tasks I dreamed up for them on my working weekends, cooperated with my plans only out of concern for their grades. And because those who planned on going to college were, with a few notable exceptions, more worried about grades than were the vocationally oriented students, they could be manipulated into a reasonable facsimile of performance, if not actual learning. However, I always taught several sections of general education students who were not as vulnerable to this sort of pressure. At that time, I did not understand the connection between control and curriculum any more than I understood the connection between curriculum and the learner.

Eventually, I learned to read between the lines which divided students into college and general education curricula. What I discovered was what Mayher (1990) calls "commonsense discrimination," which relies on standardized testing to group or track youngsters into classes based on their "ability." As Mayher is quick to point out, "socioeconomic factors do influence [students'] capacities to profit from school instruction" as well as the ways in which they are treated by teachers (1990, pp. 58-61). At Smithfield, my college preparatory students were white and, for the most part, Jewish; on the other hand, my general education students were African-Americans and ethnic Catholics. Yale accepted at least twenty Smithfield seniors annually, and a fair number also went to Harvard and other prestigious schools. The future "Yalies" and the future secretaries both studied literature.

Since Smithfield is nestled in the shadow of "Mother Yale," it was inevitable that several of my younger colleagues were graduates of Yale's Master of Arts in Teaching program. Arthur N. Applebee describes the program's well-attended conferences as offering an "academic view of English" (1974, p. 192). Of course, this approach was a reaction to the emphasis on students' personal interests, needs, and goals—known as "life adjustment"—which had been the focus of curriculum for many years and that had degenerated into the last gasp of the progressive movement. Applebee articulates this shift in focus clearly when, in summarizing the results of a 1959 conference of the American Studies Association, the College English Association, the Modern Language Association, and the National Council of Teachers of English, he says:

The most important assertion was that English must be regarded as a "fundamental liberal discipline," a body of specific knowledge to be preserved and transmitted rather than a set of skills or an opportunity for guidance and individual adjustment. As such, the importance of specific works, of the technical vocabulary of the literary critic, and of sequence determined by the logic of the subject matter could be opened for debate in a way that was impossible when the subject was defined in terms of the needs or interests of the student. College professors of English rather than of education or psychology became the body of expert opinion of most importance in curriculum development. . . . Because the basis of the curriculum was felt to lie in the subject matter, such experts could provide guidance of a nearly universally applicable sort. (1974, p. 193)

At Smithfield, we just loved "playing professor." Our pedagogy was, as I see now, right in line with the Commission on English, a body appointed by the College Entrance Examination Board in 1959 to "propose standards of achievement" and "suggest ways of meeting them" (Applebee, 1974, p. 196). This group viewed the teacher as a "'professional'—that is, as one who had himself through long exposure come to 'know' literature, and thus who, because of the depth and rigor of his training, would be able to select appropriate works and discuss them in appropriate ways" (p. 196). Applebee goes on to say that the commission advocated New Criticism as the appropriate mode of discourse about literature. Teachers were to prepare to discuss with their students questions of form, rhetoric, meaning, and, finally, value. Now I understand that granting expertise in curriculum development to college professors of any discipline meant that classroom teachers became, by default, nonexperts, condemned to only pretending to profess.

In retrospect, too, I realize that our selection of the texts that were appropriate for each grade was influenced by the ideas of Jerome Bruner (cited in Applebee, 1974). At that time, Bruner believed that "any subject [could] be taught effectively in some intellectually honest form to any child at any stage of development" (Applebee, 1974, p. 195). He chaired a conference of the National Academy of Sciences which brought together thinkers from many disciplines to consider learning, curriculum, and teaching. Not surprisingly, in his final report on the conference, Bruner envisioned a literature curriculum which, for example, can create for the student "an evermore complex and mature understanding of the nature of tragedy" (Applebee, 1974, p. 195). I taught the books in the book closet: Shakespeare, Hawthorne, Salinger, Hemingway, Dickens, Eliot, Wharton, and numerous anthologies of poetry and short stories. At Smithfield, as at many other high schools, literature was taught by genre, with a different one each quarter.

Composition meant writing critical essays about the literature we read. At the end of each quarter, I usually asked my students to write a piece in whatever genre we had been discussing. During senior year, they struggled to churn out essays to accompany their applications to college or letters to accompany their resumés. There were grammar books, but although I detailed grammar lessons in my plans, I could never bring myself to teach them. Grammar instructions for the college-bound students would have been redundant: their grammar was as good as mine. I simply edited their papers, responding to matters of style and content in what I hoped was a helpful way. For the others, I did not know what to do, since it was becoming clear to me that their dialects were somehow largely responsible for their placement in General English rather than College English classes. In the spirit of what I thought of as fairness, I edited their papers too, systematically red-penciling all their deviations from Standard English.

THE FIRST HUNDRED YEARS

Like the Hudson County Community College tutors, readers of these pages must, at times, tune out the voice of the veteran educator, and instead, strain to hear the voice of a neophyte as I resurrect her and her world on the page. To conjure up the young teacher that I was in the early 1960s, I must rely heavily on memories—memories that are as vivid as nightmares, so frequently have I relived them.

In Sandra Cisneros's *The House on Mango Street*, Esperanza, the prepubescent protagonist, has just moved into a new and rather disappointing neighborhood when she says: "Some day I will have a best friend all my own. One I can tell my secrets to. One who will understand my

jokes without my having to explain them. Until then I am
a red balloon, a balloon tied to an anchor" (1991, p. 9).

That is exactly how I felt as a first-year teacher. But
whereas Esperanza's large and close Mexican family
anchored her amid the chaos of Chicago's barrio, I was
new to New Haven, newly married, and new to teaching.
Before the school year began, all this newness had seemed
an adventure; I was confident that I would make friends,
as I always had. An extrovert in the Jungian sense, I
require the physical and psychic proximity of others,
preferably caring others, to confirm my sense of existence.
Therefore, early on I had become proficient at connecting
with people, and although I had often been bored in
classrooms, I had never been lonely in school. On the
contrary, I fully expected that as a young, idealistic, and
"liberally" educated teacher, I would be surrounded by
appreciative students, empathetic colleagues, and nurturing
mentors. It had never occurred to me that my students
would ever feel about me exactly as I had felt about my
high school English teachers.

That year at Smithfield I taught five English classes,
managed a homeroom, and monitored a study hall. My
first-period General English IV class was a group of about
thirty senior boys. I recall watching them squatting in the
corridor outside the door of room A301 on my first day,
smirking up at me. Then, still squatting, they duck-walked
past me as I stood in the doorway, poised expectantly in a
pink, pleated chemise dress. My smile of welcome froze
as their leering faces paraded by my knocking knees. They
formed a seemingly endless parade of eighteen- and
nineteen-year-old males and, as I saw when they finally
stood up, many of them were well over six feet tall, and
the shorter ones were hulking, nonetheless. I could not
believe there were no girls, but there were none. I later
learned that most of these strapping fellows were "jocks,"
athletes who played on Smithfield's championship basket-
ball and football teams; their schedules had been coordi-

nated to facilitate their early dismissal for practice. That year I also taught another senior General English class and three sophomore classes. One of the sophomore classes was a middle-level college preparatory group and the other two were made up of General English students. There was a twenty-minute lunch break in the middle of fifth period. By the afternoon of my first day, I realized that the appreciation, empathy, and nurturing I had envisioned enjoying at Smithfield would not be easy to come by.

My students that year were only occasionally appreciative; more often, they were hostile. Once I asked a senior boy who had been laughing and talking with a crony in the back row to move to a front row seat, where I hoped he would be less disruptive, only to have him ask, "What do you want me to do? Sit in the front of the room and jerk off?" Three decades later, I still flinch when I remember eighteen-year-old Thomas Abbruzzi's cryptic question, which he spat at me while he grudgingly transferred his books and body to a front-row desk.

My peers were companionable, but we were often at odds philosophically—if one can call our reactive rantings philosophy. Over innumerable cups of coffee, we rehashed each day's events. The other wives of Yale graduate students and I saw ourselves as teaching for only a few years until our husbands finished their studies. Nonetheless, we were conscientious and hard-working. Most of them had enjoyed high school English themselves and did not question Smithfield's curriculum or pedagogy, whereas I had found high school English boring and irrelevant and wondered why so little had changed.

By Christmas, Susan, a potential soulmate who was a Vassar alumna, too, as well as a graduate of the Yale Master of Arts in Teaching program, had resolved to leave Smithfield in June to teach in the suburbs. Helene's husband was soon graduating from medical school, so they planned to move. Marcia was pregnant and was not even sure she would be able to finish the year. Even Jerry, my trusted neighbor in Room A303, was applying for a vice-principalship so as to better provide for his growing family. Then, there was Kathy, who was rumored to be sexually involved with a senior boy; this both shocked and threatened me, and it made her unacceptable as a confidante. Even my husband soon tired of my endless recitations of Smithfield stories and gently but firmly declared the subject off-limits.

My more experienced colleagues were reminiscent of my own high school teachers, from whose ministrations I was still recovering. Mrs. Winebaum, a well-meaning and some what maternal history teacher, suggested that I lengthen my skirts. The football coach had his own agenda; he sent me a welcoming note via a student. It read, in part: "The boys listed below are members of the Smithfield High football team who are in your first period General English IV class. They are to receive grades of C or better in order that they remain eligible to play this season. Cordially, Joe Finch, Coach." The names of fully half the students in General English IV were listed alphabetically beneath his signature. Fortunately, Miss Nolan was willing to do battle with Coach Finch on my behalf.

Initially, I turned often to the administration for guidance and support, but Mrs. Winebaum advised me that if I sent too many discipline problems to my department head or the central office, my eventual application for tenure would be looked on unfavorably. I soon became ambivalent about administrative intervention anyway, since it was hard to imagine the authors of the dress code and the narrators of the daily harangues on the public address system as sources of justice tempered with mercy and wisdom.

On one especially memorable day, an eighteen-year-old senior named Sean O'Donnell, who was a parochial school reject, an aspiring poet, and an alcoholic, wandered into my fifth period class drunk. He staggered to the front of the room; I can still see Sean's disheveled red hair, bleary and bloodshot eyes, and rumpled, blue button-down shirt. His fly was unzipped. I was sitting near the back; the students were writing. Sean, who was not even a member of this particular class, began to mumble at his startled audience. While I debated what to do, Mr. Kelly, the vice principal, entered and sat down to observe the class. I had to decide whether to turn Sean in, setting him up for instant expulsion, or just keep quiet and pray that Mr. Kelly would mistake this Beckettesque scenario for a normal recitation. I took the latter course, and Sean's intoxicated intrusion went undetected; for better or worse, he graduated that June. Within a few years he was serving in Viet Nam.

The administration, and most notably Miss Nolan, was responsible for the requirement that nontenured English teachers write and submit weekly lesson plans every Monday morning before homeroom, a mandate that I deeply resented. These lesson plans had to include detailed study questions on reading assignments as well as plans for work in grammar, tests and quizzes, essay assignments, and discussion topics. When she "popped in" to observe us, Miss Nolan expected to find us doing exactly what we had planned. This requirement was made all the more absurd because she could not possibly read, comment on, and return the plans before the middle of the week. In those pre-Xerox days, we had to make carbon copies of our plans to use while Miss Nolan scrutinized the originals.

Composing and crafting these plans took me most of every weekend during my first year at Smithfield. The rest of the weekend was spent correcting papers. Sometime between Friday and Monday, I also wanted to clean our apartment, shop, do the laundry, and try to deconstruct *The Joy of Cooking* enough to prepare a meal or two, since I had no time to cook during the week, and we could seldom afford the available alternatives. Quite simply, I had never worked so hard for such long hours before.

Compared to my work-load at Smithfield, Vassar College
had been a vacation. I accepted my domestic lot; somebody had to cook, clean, launder, and shop, and thirty
years ago, that somebody was almost always female. But
unlike homemaking, writing those detailed lesson plans
seemed useless. Also, turning them in was demeaning; it
was clear that Miss Nolan did not trust us to plan, so we
had to produce written evidence that we did.

Unfortunately, there were seldom any enlightening
comments in response to our plans; such a reaction might
have partially justified doing them. As it was, the plan
writing seemed a big waste of time and energy, which not
only interfered with my personal life but also inhibited me
in the classroom. The plans became a kind of script which
at first I felt compelled to follow, regardless of what
interesting or productive alternatives presented themselves.
When I deviated from the script and ad-libbed, as I
eventually learned to do, I felt guilty and afraid of being
found out.

Understandably, I grew increasingly isolated, disillu-
sioned, and discouraged as the months passed. I woke up
each morning weeping at the prospect of yet another day
at Smithfield High. By the year's end, I was exhausted and
relieved. My husband got a summer job, so I registered
for a course on the contemporary French novel at Yale's
Summer Language Institute and spent July and August
reading Gide and Camus in the bathtub of our apartment,
trying to keep cool. I avoided thinking about teaching.
But with the inexorable approach of Labor Day, I faced
the prospect of another year in room A301, equipped with
lowered expectations and the past year's lesson plans ready
for recycling.

2

Teacher: Sylvia Ashton-Warner

A RETROSPECTIVE RESPONSE

Early in September 1963, just a few days after school had
started, I read Katherine Taylor's rave review of *Teacher*
by Sylvia Ashton-Warner on the front page of the *New
York Times Book Review*. The next day after school, I
stopped at the Yale Co-op and bought the book. I
remember reading it in one sitting. It did not matter to
me that Ashton-Warner lived in New Zealand, was much
older than I, and taught Maori five-year-olds instead of
urban American teenagers. I knew I was home; Sylvia
became a kind of anchor for me as I struggled to survive
and teach at Smithfield High.

In a letter to her New York publisher, which precedes
the book itself, it becomes clear that Ashton-Warner also
felt isolated from the educational establishment in her
own country. She alludes to the difficulties she experienced getting her "Creative Teaching Scheme" published
there, as well as to the accidental burning of her painstak-
ingly crafted "Transition Readers" (1963; 1986, pp. 22-25).
After reading this letter, I pictured Ashton-Warner as a
kindred spirit, another lonely, unappreciated teacher

struggling against great odds. Near the end of the letter, she notes:

I have been writing to you in pencil by the fire with the evening to myself. Meaning to correct, revise, improve, and type—and shorten—don't forget . . . tomorrow. But I can't do any of these things. I'm going to tear these pages out of this notebook and put them in an envelope tomorrow, to be posted over the Pacific[,] . . . never to read again. Don't fear they are too rough to publish; with or without punctuation and polish; backwards, upside-down or down-side up my readers will know what I mean. (1986, p. 26)

She was right. I, her reader, knew exactly what she meant. Before I even began her book, I was seduced by her passion, her impetuosity, and the romantic image of the solitary teacher-writer, pencil scrawling furiously, silhouetted against the fire.

In retrospect, it is clear that Ashton-Warner's writing style had a great deal to do with her appeal to me when I was twenty-three. According to linguist George Lakoff and philosopher Mark Johnson, "New metaphors are capable of creating new understandings and, therefore, new realities" (1980, p. 235). Through Ashton-Warner's Freudian imagery, teaching becomes "espousal," during which her pupils "become part of me, like a lover. The approach, little different. The askance observation first, the acceptance next, then the gradual or quick coming, until in the complete procuration, there glows the harmony, the peace" (1986, pp. 210-11). My professors at Vassar had been experts, sharing with their students the results of their scholarship. Mrs. Winebaum had told me that teaching was like training animals, and Jerry, relying on his navy experience, had said it was like training recruits. At Smithfield, I could be expert only to those few who valued the knowledge I offered. I was failing in the big top and on the aircraft carrier, but as a recent bride, I still felt optimistic about espousal. In 1963, on the threshold of the long overdue sexual revolution, Ashton-Warner's determination to see teaching as an organic, life-affirming process that resulted in "a long, perpetuating, never-ending, transmuting birth" was a joyous relief to me (1986, p. 211).

And there was more about her writing to which, as a beginning teacher, I could immediately respond. She addresses her readers, whom she envisions as nursery school teachers, directly, and she also includes dialogue, photos, drawings, and classroom anecdotes as well as personal stories. Moreover, Ashton-Warner refers frequently to her extensive readings in psychology, history, and literature. By doing so, she reaffirmed my sense of what it meant to be educated, for I believed then in the power of the word to change the world. To be educated was to be well-read: this view had been reinforced and refined by my years as an English major at Vassar. Ashton-Warner not only knew about pedagogy and children, but she valued the arts and quoted Plato, Da Vinci, and Tolstoy along with Freud and Jung.

Even more impressive, she had written a novel, *Spinster* (1959), which had actually been published and widely read. I admired published writers even more than I admired voracious readers. My most positive memories of high school have to do with writing for the newspaper there, and I secretly cherished the dream of writing a novel of my own someday. Ashton-Warner seemed, not only like the best friend and traveling companion I needed, but also like the successful teacher-writer I wanted to be. And she had done all this while married and rearing a family. I was both comforted and inspired.

Cross-Cultural Companion

Teacher moved me for other reasons too. It was published several years before the 1966 summer seminar at

Dartmouth College where fifty British and American specialists in English struggled with the legacies of Locke and Dewey in an effort to determine the direction of teaching practice. Nevertheless, in *Teacher*, Ashton-Warner reconstrues the traditional Lockean concept of knowledge as a transmittable entity to be channeled from the all-knowing teacher to the know-nothing student. Ashton-Warner's description of the workings of her organic method of teaching reading best exemplifies how revolutionary her pedagogy was. As Phillida Salmon points out in her discussion of cross-cultural teaching: "In daring to hear these children, to relate personally to them, Ashton-Warner managed to grasp something of their real experience. It was in the end, her affirmation of this experience, by making it the curriculum of her teaching, which proved the turning point of the children's learning to read" (1986, p. 45).

In her organic pedagogy, Ashton-Warner exploits what she calls the inner vision of the children, their personal constructs of reality. To do so, she explains, she "reach[es] a hand into the mind of the child, bring[s] out a handful of the stuff [she] find[s] there, and use[s] that as their first working material" (1986, p. 34). This "stuff," which is highly charged with personal and cultural meaning, and includes words like "Mummy," "Daddy," "kiss," "frightened," and "ghost," becomes the child's customized "Key Vocabulary." She writes such one-word captions for the children's mental images on cards which each child first traces with a finger and then keeps as treasured objects for study.

Later Ashton-Warner has the children spell their words and combine them into sentences and stories which they read to partners, thus teaching themselves and each other. In this way, Ashton-Warner successfully incorporates the highly social and communal aspects of Maori culture into her pedagogy (1986, p. 104). Ashton-Warner elicits each child's daily Key Vocabulary word in a conference, making sure that the work is meaningful to the child; she remarks that "A five[-year-old], meeting words for the first time and finding out that they have intense meaning for him, at once loves reading" (1986, p. 70). For this reason, she rejects the white "Janet and John" reading primers and ultimately creates her own "Transition Readers," using familiar vocabulary and Maori themes to which her pupils easily relate and which bridge the chasm between the two diverse languages and cultures.

My college preparatory students and I spoke the same language and came from the same middle-class Jewish, or other Euro-American, background. They were willing to plod through the canonical classics, as I had in high school, simply because they wanted to get into college, just as I had. I was, in fact, a useful role model for these students since I had done what they wanted to do: attend a "good" college and graduate. With my ponytail and miniskirt, I was an attractive and enthusiastic advocate of literature, literary criticism, art films, poetry, and drama. I managed to be entertaining and demanding at the same time, spending hours responding to their essays and planning their work. Our biggest problems arose over grades ("Mrs. I, why did I only get a B+ on that test?") and occasional cheating.

But my General English students and I spoke different languages and represented different cultures and, often, different social classes. I remember an essay in which Willie Simpson described Macbeth as a "jelly belly jive pig." I loved the sound and image conjured up by Willie's Key Vocabulary, but what did he mean? And how should I respond? Willie's grammar was also nonstandard, so I was constantly editing his verbs and double negatives with my relentless red pen. Linguists had yet to acknowledge or describe Black English, but students like Willie were speaking and writing it—and teachers like me were correcting it.

Nancy Polanski was a bright and sensitive student in one of my senior General English classes; she invited me to her wedding, which she had spent much of her senior year planning. I went because I liked her and wished her well, and in spite of the fact that I had spent much of the year trying to convince her to delay her marriage and consider the possibility of going to college. I was so much a product of my own education-oriented class and culture that I did not readily recognize or value those of others. (My desire for Nancy to go to college was not a prefeminist reaction on my part, but rather a manifestation of my belief that one could be a better wife and mother if one went to college first.)

Similarly, I remember agreeing to do homebound instruction with Cecile Murray, a pregnant sixteen-year-old student in one of my junior General English classes. (In those days, pregnant teens withdrew from school and were tutored at home.) Again, I liked her and wished her well, but I could not fathom why, as an intelligent young woman, she had allowed herself to become sexually active, let alone pregnant, at sixteen. During our weekly sessions at her flat in a run-down neighborhood, I was struck by the bare floorboards and neat but sparse furnishings. I met Cecile's mother, a warm and energetic woman in her thirties who would soon be a grandmother. As Cecile and I discussed *Romeo and Juliet* and sipped Cokes, I tried to fit the Murray's growing family into my construct of family. I wondered how reading *Romeo and Juliet* was going to help Cecile cope with an infant. I felt as if I were a tourist in a foreign country. I wondered what literature Ashton-Warner would have recommended to Willie, Nancy, and Cecile, and how, for each, she would have woven their disparate backgrounds and cultures into a customized, organic language-learning experience.

Control, Community, and Conscience

Ashton-Warner's attitude toward control in the Maori nursery school where she presides is, not surprisingly, an outgrowth of her appreciation of the organic way in which children learn, as well as a reflection of her Freudian orientation. She explains that in children's minds, "the strongest impulses push up, irrespective of whether or not they should, at a given time. Making the behaviour of children anything but an ordered one in the conscious meaning of the term order" (1986, p. 97). Her admonition, "If you don't like noise, don't be a teacher!" (1986, p. 104) was reassuring to me as I tried to find ways to maintain a semblance of peace, if not control, in room A301.

At the beginning of the 1960s, Ashton-Warner made explicit for me, for the first time, the connection between the larger community and the tone of the classroom. She describes a Maori district in which she once taught in this way: "The district itself had tone. The people had sitting among them authentic leaders and all remained well. There was serenity. It flowed down . . . like the influence of a headmaster through his school" (1986, p. 86). I began to read the *New Haven Register* as well as the *New York Times* to try to piece together some sense of the several worlds that made up New Haven at that time.

I also began to reach out to the parents. Again, in the case of my college preparatory students, they usually got to me first, calling me at home, flocking in on Parents' Night, and, in general, acting like my parents had. I was happy to conspire with these parents to "motivate" their kids. The parents of my general education students were another matter, however. A fair number did come to school, but I was not very adept at communicating with them, especially as I realized that many of them took me and school very seriously.

A particularly troubling parental encounter occurred with Mr. Piascack, Andrew's father. Andrew was a burly eighteen-year-old youth who was often a nuisance. He liked attention, and he didn't like *Macbeth*. On Parents' Night, I told his father that Andrew frequently disrupted our class and asked him to speak with Andrew about this behavior. Mr. Piascack promised to do so, and the next day, Andrew came in subdued but stony-faced and hostile. After class, he explained that his dad had beaten him brutally with a strap as punishment for his antics in school. Andrew never interrupted a class again, but he never smiled again either. I felt awful. Yes, in 1963 I was interested to note that, like me, Ashton-Warner is not always effective in channeling the destructive impulses of some of the young Maori warriors and maidens. When she does raise her voice or send a youngster to the headmaster for discipline, she, too, pays for it with a night of anguish over how she might better have handled the situation (1986, p. 131). She has few illusions about her own capacity for rage and is careful to allow it to spend itself before she touches a child.

Artist or Drone

Although I relished almost every word of *Teacher*, there was one part that was especially validating and significant to me during the next two years at Smithfield. Ashton-Warner devotes several impassioned pages to the proposition that good teachers should not need or use workbooks, by which she means written lesson plans. She goes so far as to reiterate the argument of teachers who depend on written lesson plans: "I can't rely on myself in the melee of a lesson to work out sequences on the spot. When the time comes I need everything at my finger tips. I've got to have it all thought out beforehand" (1986, p. 88). She then juxtaposes this view with her notion of a planbook as a "middleman, intercepting some of the energy and glamour directed upon the canvas" of the artist. And, make no mistake, Ashton-Warner clearly sees teachers as artists for whom the "middleman" of workbooks is intrusive and unnecessary:

It doesn't always, I think, clarify a teacher's thoughts to note them down. To some it's pinioning. Something to evade. I learned when I was a very small girl that you could leave half your meaning behind in a preparatory sketch. When I was very young I worked straight from my mind upon the clay. Then I knew what I did was all of what I could do and not just the residue of a trial. And when in teaching I found that I was required to precede all my work with the written notes of a workbook, it was with gross payment to the middleman that I did so. . . . How are we to know what is going to come from the children on this day or that? (1986, p. 89)

I definitely felt pinioned by Miss Nolan's insistence that we write, submit, and follow weekly lesson plans. Although I didn't stop writing my plans when I read *Teacher,* for I hoped to be tenured, I was enormously reassured to learn that we artists did not really need them.

Likewise, it was comforting to read of Ashton-Warner's concern about observations and evaluations of her performance in the classroom and to learn that, at least once, she had actually received a poor rating: "We had our grading this week. The men were well marked, Tom and K., but as usual I was very low. There's no doubt about it. I am a very low ability teacher" (1986, p. 119). Another time, when contemplating an impending inspection, which she has every reason to believe will go well, she says:

I'm very nervous. . . . It's no good anybody telling me not to be nervous. There's a ghoul from the past that haunts, I think, all teachers of my generation. . . . If *only* I had the confidence of being a good teacher. But I'm not even an appalling teacher. I don't even claim to be a teacher at all. I'm just a nitwit somehow let loose among children. (1986, p. 198)

I appreciated Ashton-Warner's willingness to acknowledge

her anxiety before being observed. This revelation made it easier to bear Miss Nolan's criticism, as well as my ongoing self-doubts.

Ashton-Warner's self-doubts often resulted in modifications to her pedagogy and philosophy; in fact, they were the initial stages of her productive and satisfying classroom research, for her Organic Teaching Scheme is the product of years of careful observation and experimentation. In room A301 at Smithfield, I, too, had many doubts about who I was and what I was doing; at times, these doubts seemed overwhelming, reducing me to bouts of nocturnal weeping. Like Alice's, my progress was often made more difficult as I floundered about in pools of my own tears. I felt my personality and identity eroding as I yelled at the students, kowtowed to the administration, and argued with my colleagues. It is small wonder that reading *Teacher* was a watershed experience for me. After finishing Ashton-Warner's story, I very gradually and tentatively began to consider the possibility that it might be alright to have more questions than answers and to look for the answers in my own classroom rather than in advice from peers and colleagues. Joseph P. McDonald (1992) describes Ashton-Warner as "the poet of reflective practice. One reads her today for her modeling of a teacher's self-scrutiny. Her value is less in what she reports finding in this self-scrutiny and more in the example of her daring to undertake it, her demonstration of how to do it" (p. 113).

One spring day, while holding a desultory discussion of the short story "The Lottery" with the other three people in the sophomore General English class who had read it, I had an epiphany. I stopped the class and asked my apathetic and unprepared students to, right then and there, read the story and make up their own questions suitable for using as study questions. I asked for no answers—just questions. They began to work, and I collected the questions the next day when the class reconvened. I then selected one student to pose her questions to the class and

call on people to answer them. Immediately, the dynamic
of the ensuing discussion changed. Many more people
were now prepared and eager to participate. Many were
also eager to play teacher and challenge their classmates.
Each day, someone different volunteered. I collected and
reviewed the study questions every night. True, I had
more paperwork to do, but I no longer had to make up
questions on the reading and then answer most of them
myself.

The success of this simple and rather primitive step
toward what I recognize now as a reallocation of power
and responsibility in room A301 went a long way to boost
my flagging morale as the end of my second teaching year
finally drew near. It was for me the equivalent of what
classroom researcher Patricia J. Sikes calls a "critical
incident" in the life of a beginning teacher (1985, p. 33).
However, although the episodes that Sikes describes are
centered around disciplinary confrontations, my incident
was curriculum-based and only affected my students'
behavior secondarily. It was important for me to make
concrete my conviction that as student involvement and
investment in classwork increased, there would be fewer
interruptions and distractions.

Ashton-Warner's moving account of her own progres-
sion from doubting to doing helped me stop whining to
others and start teaching. In her biography of Ashton-
Warner, Linley Hood notes the enormous and nearly
universal appeal of *Teacher*:

Teacher, with its impressionistic fragments and emotive prose,
was not a conventional teaching text[,] . . . but *Teacher* was as
gripping to Sylvia's supporters as the key words had been to her
five year olds: one read and they were hooked. So what if it's
emotional? So what if it's unscientific? In these qualities lie its
strength. To teachers and parents who longed for a more
humane and creative world, Sylvia Ashton-Warner was a hero.
For thousands of readers, *Teacher* affirmed the truths they held
most dear and gave them the courage to translate those truths

into action. Yet the uniqueness of each person's truth meant that the book revealed a different message to every reader. (1988, p. 176)

Hood describes the book's significance to teachers who are creative, teachers of reading, artistic, unconventional teachers, or unappreciated teachers, as well as those readers who are concerned with communication and mental health. In addition, according to Hood, Ashton-Warner had a large and active following among those educators who opposed the "basal-reader empire." At least, in my appreciation of *Teacher* I was not alone.

TEACHER REVISITED

Teacher continues to engage readers. In her introduction to the 1986 edition, Maxine Hong Kingston writes, "Every September, every teacher proceeds into foreign territories—to which this book is a field guide" (p. 9). I agree. The work remains a valuable resource for first-time travelers as well as for those of us who may be a little road-weary. My new copy of *Teacher* is richly embellished with marginalia. One of my recent responses to the book was to note Ashton-Warner's incorporation of the tenets of collaborative learning into her Organic Teaching Scheme. As I mentioned earlier, she often pairs the children to work independently of her on reading, writing, and spelling (1986, p. 63). They also sit in circles to share their stories (p. 65). The ensuing discussions are "passionate interchange[s] of talk" (p. 66), uninterrupted by the teacher and free of the demands of praise and the shame of blame. They are the kind of exchanges of which Mayher speaks when he explains:

While we can learn much about content and thinking processes by listening to others, we do so much more effectively in a system that permits open give-and-take among equals than we do in a context where our major learning task is to try and memorize and be able to recall a teacher's monologues. . . . The process of engaging in such dialogues is the fundamental process through which we further develop and enrich our language system. (1990, p. 242)

Ashton-Warner's brand of collaboration results also in what has recently been dubbed "feminist" pedagogy. For when the "commonsense" (Mayher, 1990) hierarchical configurations of the traditional classroom with its rows of seats and the prominently situated teacher's desk are transformed into the dyads and circles of collaboration, the stage is set for a pedagogy of "caring" much like that advocated by Nel Noddings in *Caring: A Feminine Approach to Ethics and Moral Education* (1984). Here she describes a transaction between a caring teacher and a student:

When a teacher asks a question in class and a student responds, she receives not just the "response" but the student. What he says matters, whether it is right or wrong, and she probes gently for clarification, interpretation, contribution. She is not seeking the answer but the involvement of the cared-for. For the brief interval of dialogue that grows around the question, the cared-for indeed "fills the firmament." The student is infinitely more important than the subject matter. (p. 176)

In the course of the evolution of her or his Key Vocabulary, every youngster has a personal conversation with Ashton-Warner in which she delicately and deftly tries to elicit the semantic seeds crucial to each child's developing literacy. She tries to help each one find the words that will unlock the door to her or his emotional and lived experience and so be the "key" to future word recognition and vocabulary development.

Another aspect of Ashton-Warner's experience that is illuminated by feminist considerations is her aversion to written lesson plans. According to Grumet (1988), our docile preparation of these schemes, which we know we will then abandon in favor of more "contextual and idiosyncratic" classroom activities, is a costly capitulation to a patriarchal system. It is costly because, since we abandon the written plans in favor of "a more contextual, idiosyncratic curriculum" of our own devising, the administrative theory that the plans embody exists only on paper, while the actual practice of the teacher seldom becomes the basis for theory (p. 25). Also of significance is the fact that this "complicity" with "paternal authority" (Miss Nolan, in my case) sustains the hierarchical and bureaucratic organization of the schools. Such a perspective makes especially meaningful Ashton-Warner's determination to record and publish the theories that drove her practice.

While engaged in helping her students build linguistic bridges from the Maori *pa* (or village) to the dominant culture in New Zealand, Ashton-Warner practices the best form of bilingual education. She argues for her transitional readers by saying:

However good a book is it can't supply the transitional needs unless it is in sympathy with the Maori children, has incident which they understand and temperament which they sense. Only in a familiar atmosphere can reading be evolutionary, in much the same way as the Key Vocabulary is organic, and it is to supply these needs that the . . . Transitional Books have been composed. (1986, p. 70)

When reading Ashton-Warner's description of her "Infant Room," one visits a progressive classroom, warts and all. I now recognize her teaching as a potpourri, including whole language, process writing, reader response, collaborative learning, classroom research, a multicultural curriculum, and caring, individualized instruction. That all of these were part of the daily experience of her small charges so many years ago in New Zealand is admirable and a cause for wonder; that they are there for us now to revisit and discuss is cause for celebration.

However, the experience of rereading *Teacher* at a later point in my teaching career triggered an additional response in me that bears examination. As I read the book this time, sprawled on a blanket in a park in the special tranquility of summer study, I was moved by a section in which Ashton-Warner speaks of the necessity for creating "reciprocal respect" between teacher and student "in spite of the unrest in the tribe and the lack of cohesion in the pa and the 'fire that on my bosom preys'" (1986, pp. 86-87). She elaborates on the resulting "precarious sense of some deep order":

And then when you come to think about it, you find that of the two kinds of order, the conscious and the unconscious order, only one is real. It's the order in the deep hidden places. And whatever the temperament of the teacher and of the children, it is accessible to anyone. When we trace beyond the area of temperament and beyond the climate of the personality to its origin, we find that it is simply this order. The true order in the depths, the "still centre." (1986, p. 87)

I remember the book falling to my blanket as I lowered my head onto my folded arms and reflected on what, if any, sort of "still centre" I had possessed in 1963. It is painful to recall what a jumbled product of my class, culture, and particular parentage I had been. Now, I am aware of the enormous influence of these phenomena and have managed to forge them, together with my own felt experience, into some sort of identity, a "still centre," if you will, which is fragile, but real.

However, in retrospect, the first part of my own teaching journey was complicated or enriched, depending on how I look at it, by the identity crisis I was experiencing as I tried to come of age. For me, the passage from girlhood to womanhood took many years and was largely unconscious. It was shaped by the fact that I had, by virtue of my marriage, become a breadwinner. How could this be? Was I retracing segments of my mother's journey?

   After graduating from a three year program in teacher preparation at what was then called a normal school, my mother had become an exemplary and enthusiastic "commonsense" (Mayher, 1990) elementary school teacher in Newark, New Jersey. Following her marriage, she had taught until I was born, whereupon she could assume her "real" responsibilities of full-time wife- and motherhood. When I was in high school, she returned to Newark to teach, but found she could not. She struggled for three years to apply the strategies that had been so effective with the middle-class white children she had taught in the 1930s to the largely African-American children who lived in the housing project that supplied her school with students in the 1950s, but these children were less cooperative and less engaged.   One, Harold Jones, drew pictures of horses instead of printing his name on the lined paper she gave him. Harold was also partial to the "F" word. My mother could not understand him.

   Besides, her salary was raising our tax bracket, and my father wanted her home, anyway. It was important for her to be available to attend the luncheons held by assorted local women's organizations as an adjunct to his campaign for political office.   An attorney, he was completing a three-year term as municipal court judge and was planning to run for commissioner. *He* was the breadwinner. In her analysis of Kim Chernin's study of mother/daughter relationships in *The Hungry Self* (1985), Grumet finds Chernin "explor[ing] the daughter's identification with her mother's experience of stasis, frustration, and disappointment. She sees daughters struggling with their sense of their mothers' unrealized ambitions, unexpressed talents. So the daughter . . . may be attempting . . . to compensate her mother for her disappointments by achieving what was denied to her" (1988, p. 26). Nonetheless, years later, as I reminisced in the warm summer sunshine, I remembered the enormous ambivalence I had felt over supporting myself and my husband even temporarily. As sociologist Wini Breines succinctly phrases it in *Young, White, and Miserable: Growing Up Female in the Fifties* (1992), I had not been socialized to work (p. 74).

And there were myriad other confusions, too. For example, I had very much wanted the approval of the teacher and the judge who had reared me, even when they were personified by Miss Nolan, my Department Head, or Mr. Schwartzman, Smithfield's Principal. On the other hand, I still wanted to rebel against their strictures, which had often been unreasonable.

When I left off these musings on my own past, I realized the power of the biographical influences and developing personality of the young teacher. Even the snippets of autobiographical data I have related here are sufficient to give rise to questions of how I saw teaching, African-Americans, male and female roles, authority, convention, class, and marriage. Later, in my exploration of autobiographical writing by teachers, I was not surprised to find researcher J. Gary Knowles saying:

All the case study findings support the notion that biography is important for understanding the formation of a teacher role identity and thinking about classroom practice. Student teachers, and subsequently beginning teachers, do not enter preservice programmes like empty vessels waiting to be filled with the skills, aptitudes, and experiences appropriate for a first year teacher. Neither do they begin full time teaching with only the experience of student teaching and the university. Rather they have been subjected to a lifetime of "teacher educa-tion." . . . Personal biography seems to have profound effects on what occurs in the individual's classroom and the concept of teacher role identity is central for understanding the process by which prior experiences are transformed into classroom practice. (1992, p. 126)

In fact, even a cursory consideration of Sylvia Ashton-

Warner's own life, as she recounts it in her autobiography
(1979) and as Linley Hood describes it in her biography
(1988), reveals that Ashton-Warner, too, experienced
conflict and confusion that had its genesis in her culture
and family of origin and that greatly affected her personal
and professional relationships. Over the years I have
worked with many young teachers who reminded me very
much of myself as I had been all those years ago, with my
life and values yet unexamined and my developing self yet
uncentered, unstilled.

3

Up the Down Staircase: Bel Kaufman

A RETROSPECTIVE RESPONSE

If Sylvia Ashton-Warner's *Teacher* was a mentor's manual, Bel Kaufman's novel was a comic-book mirror in which I saw myself and my new world reflected and which revealed that world to others who did not share it. Clearly, teaching at Smithfield had become a mission to a bizarre and exotic land, and as I talked or wrote letters about the Munchkins and Lilliputians I encountered there, increasingly my tales inspired either disbelief or, worse, boredom among my friends studying in graduate school or doling out graham crackers to toddlers. But then, in 1964, Bel Kaufman's *Up the Down Staircase* was published, and everybody read about the adventures of Sylvia Barrett. Now, my stories were better understood and validated in the eyes of my friends and family.

In her funny and thought-provoking book, Kaufman chronicles the traumas and triumphs of new teacher Sylvia Barrett at Calvin Coolidge, a typically overcrowded and understaffed New York City secondary school. She does this by weaving together Barrett's letters to friends, copies of memos, student writing of various sorts, lesson plans, excerpts from report cards and permanent records, minutes of faculty meetings, and even the contents of Barrett's wastebasket. In fact, the book is an extension of an article, "From a Teacher's Wastebasket," which Kaufman wrote in 1962 after fifteen years of teaching. There is the barest hint of a plot as the reader shares Barrett's concerns for particular students as well as her own sanity and professional future. One of the novel's central questions is whether Barrett will return to Calvin Coolidge the following year or accept a position at Willowdale Academy, a small women's college in a bucolic setting where three days a week she would teach Freshman Composition and a seminar in Chaucer, her area of special study, to eight students.

Not only did *Up the Down Staircase* increase my credibility among friends and relatives, it was also a catalyst for community building at Smithfield. Indeed, regardless of pedagogical style, philosophical stance, age, or discipline, faculty members passed around a dog-eared copy of the hardback edition and chortled together over some passages that we actually read aloud in the lunchroom. The reason for the book's popularity was not so much that everyone identified with the protagonist, Sylvia Barrett; rather, it was that everyone recognized in Maxwell E. Clarke and James J. McHabe, Calvin Coolidge's principal and vice-principal, the personae of our very own Jacob S. Schwartzman and Timothy Kelly, Smithfield's leader and his lieutenant, respectively. In addition, we recognized the language, customs, rites, and rituals of Calvin Coolidge, for they, too, were very similar to those of Smithfield.

While the pedagogy and curriculum at Smithfield were teacher-centered, commonsensical, and canonical, the culture and constraints were downright bizarre. In addition to the tyranny of the eight-period day and the quarterly marking periods, the manufacture of lesson plans, biased tracking that perpetuated segregation, and the ongoing crises of control, there was the dress code. Mr. Schwartzman insisted that boys wear jackets and ties. Worse yet, failure to do so earned a student an F for that day in every class regardless of how brilliantly he performed or how warm it inevitably was in June and September. The fate of a young man who chose to make a sartorial or political statement by wearing a hat in school was similarly grim. Still worse, a teacher's failure to enforce the dress code earned a threatening reprimand and lecture from Miss Nolan or Mr. Schwartzman.

There was more. Mr. Schwartzman spoke in deep, measured tones; this would have been an advantage had he been revealing the Ten Commandments from Mount Sinai or announcing the end of the world, but he was usually just notifying us of schedule changes or reminding us to fill out forms. Furthermore, he never used one short word where he could use two or three long ones, and he never phrased any sentiment himself for which a ready cliché existed. Of course, his efforts at statesmanlike authority inevitably resulted in long pompous monologues; when the public address system clicked on during homeroom every morning, a collective groan echoed throughout the building.

Small wonder, then, that we relished the following treat from Maxwell E. Clarke:

I wish to take this opportunity to extend a warm welcome to all faculty and staff, and the sincere hope that you have returned from a healthful and fruitful summer vacation with renewed vim and vigor, ready to gird your loins and tackle the many important and vital tasks that lie ahead undaunted. Thank you for your help and cooperation. (Kaufman, 1964, p. 35)

We also guffawed in recognition at the stream of memos issuing from James J. McCabe. A typical one is:

At the end of the homeroom period, please send to me those students who have failed to report for checkout because they have left the building. (1964, p. 47)

Kaufman also satirizes the miserable lot of homeroom

teachers; the idiosyncracies of high school librarians; the endless and pointless clerical work; the dearth of supplies, desks, and lockers; and the demeaning nature of some forms of supervision. And just as Barrett, the neophyte protagonist, gradually learns the language and customs of Calvin Coolidge, so does the reader gradually form an impression of Barrett.

An Alter Ego to Examine

To me in 1964, Sylvia Barrett was useful in the way that fictional characters often are. She offered me the chance to examine my own experience indirectly by looking at hers; at twenty-four, my capacity for introspection was often limited, literally running to questions like, "What's a nice Jewish girl like me doing in a place like this?" Or "Why is somebody who's smart and educated having so much trouble with this job?" Waxing philosophical after a particularly bad day, I might go so far as to roll my eyes heavenward and whine, "Why me?"

It was easier to think about Sylvia Barrett. Why was *she* teaching? She didn't even have a husband in graduate school. However, in a letter to her college friend Ellen, written on September 7, she writes:

While you are strolling through your suburban supermarket with your baby in the cart, or taking a shower in the middle of third period, I am automatically erasing "Fuck Teacher" from the blackboard.

What I really had in mind was to do a little teaching. "And gladly wolde he lerne and gladly teche"—like Chaucer's Clerk of Oxenford. I had come eager to share all I know and feel; to imbue the young with a love for their language and literature; to instruct and inspire. (Kaufman, 1964, p. 41)

Thus, the reader realizes that Barrett had aspired to teach, to transmit, if you will, her knowledge and interests to young people, a worthy enough goal at the time and one that embodies and confirms the metaphors for teaching that I cited in chapter 1.

Barrett frequently alludes to Ellen's domestic and maternal life-style, sympathizing with the difficulties she faces in selecting a color scheme for her living room or congratulating Ellen on her baby's first tooth. At times she wonders about Rhoda, a friend who left college prior to graduation and who now works "writing advertising copy for a cosmetics firm at three times my salary" (Kaufman, 1964, p. 53). These musings reveal the relative simplicity and/or shallowness of her peers' lives in contrast to her own zealous struggle, which is alive with purpose and marked by Sturm und Drang.

By the time I had read *Up the Down Staircase*, I had distanced myself a little from the trauma of my first year at Smithfield and was beginning to experience, ever so tentatively, some of the profession's rewards. One of these was that I was never bored; I envied the Ellens and Rhodas in my life their financial security, but I did not want to be a twenty-four-year-old suburban matron or a drone toiling in a publishing company. I was slowly learning to appreciate the steady stream of different human beings with whom I came in contact every day.

Sylvia Barrett's reflections on her education for her chosen profession interested me also. Like me, she considered herself ill-prepared for high school teaching. In her letter of September 7, after only one day in the classroom, Barrett tries to describe Calvin Coolidge:

It's a far cry from our dorm in Lyons Hall; a far cry from the sheltered Graduate School Library stacks; a far cry from Chaucer; and a far and desperate cry from Education 114 and Professor Winters' lectures on the "Psychology of the Adolescent." I have met the adolescent face to face; obviously, Prof. Winters had not. (Kaufman, 1964, p. 41)

Keeping Barrett company for a while clarified for me the

inadequacies of my own preparation for teaching. Unlike me, though, Barrett had a mentor to mother her through the unique passage that is professional apprenticeship. Veteran teacher Bea Schacter, a widow with no children, enfolds the younger woman under her expansive wings, nurturing and supporting the neophyte's personal and professional development.

A Mentor in the Madness

To Barrett, Schacter serves as translator: "'Keep on file in numerical order' means throw in wastebasket" (Kaufman, 1964, p. 24); advisor: "Sit on them from the first moment to show you're boss; they can find out later how nice you really are" (p. 36); companion: "Can we synchronize our lunch periods?" (p. 230); and role model extraordinaire. Schacter is the one who interrupts the flow of trivia at faculty meetings to bring up matters such as "the burden of the teaching load, clerical work, and inadequate facilities," as well as student dropouts and integration (Kaufman, p. 1964, 69). She is often late in responding to Barrett's memos because she is persuading a "salvageable kid not to drop out of school" or straightening out another one's schedule (p. 39). During Christmas vacation she takes a group of students who have never been to a theatrical performance to see some off-Broadway shows (p. 310).

In the lunchroom where the faculty members are reacting to the death of a student who tried to induce an abortion with a knitting needle, it is Schacter who speaks of love, saying that the children are starved for it and that detachment is impossible for the teachers, who "must teach—against all odds, against all obstacles, in the best sense of the word" (Kaufman, 1964, p. 175). Schacter, who no longer struggles with the issues of identity and isolation that mark early adulthood, has reached the generative stage of life, which Erikson defines as, in part, concerned with guiding the next generation (1968, p. 138).

The twenty-four-year-old neophyte that I was at Smithfield was inspired by this impassioned exhortation from the seasoned veteran at the front. For a time, in my imagination Bea Schacter rivaled Sylvia Ashton-Warner as the "mother of all mentors." In fact, she was helpful in enabling me to recognize a real-life mentor when one finally materialized the following year in the form of an innovative and inspiring social studies teacher at Smithfield, Rhonda Gold.

Schacter was also useful to me as I inadvertently became a mentor by default to members of the annual crop of new English teachers who found their way to Smithfield in the early 1960s. By September 1965 I had been granted tenure, becoming one of the youngest "senior" members of our department. I was assigned the top-level college preparatory classes as well as the newly formed experimental remedial reading groups. As I navigated my way carefully between these polar extremes, newer neophytes actually looked to me for advice and support as they confronted the tyrannies of the dress code and the lesson plan. I felt like a tour guide in a country I had visited only briefly and where the nuances of the language and customs were still somewhat alien to me. But I no longer had to submit my weekly lesson plans to Miss Nolan, I no longer broke into a cold sweat in June when I "forgot" to fail the tieless, and I no longer greeted each new day with tears.

Cupid in the Classroom

Barrett's adventures at Calvin Coolidge dramatized a very complex issue that bothered me as a young teacher: the matter of my own emerging identity. My ongoing identity crisis was immeasurably complicated by issues related to gender. I am convinced that one of the reasons why *Up the Down Staircase* was so popular was that it is a classroom drama that juxtaposes a young, pretty, warmhearted, and incurably middle-class teacher with one young student who is handsome, cynical, and incurably "hoody." I had Thomas Abbruzzi; Barrett has Joe Ferone. Joe Ferone is a chronic truant and troublemaker who has resisted her best efforts to manipulate, charm, or persuade him into even a semblance of appropriate behavior in school, despite the fact that he is intelligent. He has suffered at home and on the street, and finds school irrelevant to his problems, so his rebellion and cynicism are not without cause.

In response to a message from Barrett, Ferone finally agrees to an after-school conference. Kaufman's description of the meeting gives it the air of a tryst, in preparation for which Barrett has donned her signature red suit and freshened her lipstick. Ferone makes a late entrance; he, too, has "spruced himself up" (Kaufman, 1964, p. 312). The school is deserted; the stage is set. In a letter to Ellen, Barrett describes how, swaggering toward her with his leather jacket unzipped, a menacing Ferone reveals his sexual interpretation of her previous attentions and kindnesses to him, as well as of her frequent requests to meet with him alone (p. 313). During this encounter, Barrett is literally backed up against a wall, whereupon she shifts the situation by reaching out to touch the face of the conflicted young man. "Only my touch could speak. I care, it said, I do care" (p. 314). Cursing her, Ferone leaves, while Barrett collapses in tears at her desk.

It is easy to write off this scene as Kaufman's deliberate effort to inject the potential for sex and violence into the novel, but I do not wish to do so. Rather, Barrett is convinced that, for a moment, her touch reduces the distance she has created between herself and her student. Likewise, she tells Ellen that this distance "kept me safe from feeling" (Kaufman, 1964, p. 315). She goes on to exclaim:

> But for a moment, or hour, or whatever measure of time it takes
> to grow, we reached each other, Ferone and I, person to person.
> For love is growth. It is the ultimate commitment. It im-
> poses obligations; it risks pain. Love is what I wanted from all
> . . . but I had never really loved back. And maybe now I can.
> Ferone taught me. Our roles became reversed. He had
> reached *me*. I was the one who needed *him*, to make me feel.
> (Kaufman, 1964, pp. 315-16)

Barrett speaks passionately about the "burden of love
for all the Ferones waiting for me in the classroom," a
burden she feels is too great (p. 316). But then, as if to
reject this rather pat and simplistic view of what transpired
between her and Ferone, Barrett goes on:

> I had set out to tell you exactly what happened. But since I am
> the one writing this, how do I know what in my telling I am
> selecting, omitting, emphasizing; what unconscious editing I am
> doing? Why was I more interested in the one black sheep (I use
> Ferone's own cliché) than in all the white lambs in my care?
> Why did I (in my red suit) call him a child? (p. 316)

Here Barrett models the kind of reflection in which I
needed to engage; her questions about her own motives
and behavior as a teacher, a woman, and a writer were
reassuring to me since I constantly asked myself similar
ones. And I had no doubt that her responses to Ferone
are indeed influenced to some extent by the fact that she
finds him attractive and has unconsciously flirted with him.
This incident is counterbalanced by a parallel episode in
which Alice Blake, a sensitive young student, falls in love
with her English teacher, Paul Barringer, an alcoholic
would-be writer who is the English department's resident
Lothario. After much mooning and deliberation, and full
of hope, which was fed, like Ferone's, by need and coinci-
dence, Alice leaves Barringer a love letter on his desk

which he reads, corrects for syntax and grammar, and
returns to her. Devastated, Alice attempts suicide by
throwing herself out of his classroom window. At the
novel's end, she remains hospitalized, and Barringer still
believes that he handled her love letter "in the only way
possible" (Kaufman, 1964, p. 250).

With a worldview still unframed by feminism, and
equally innocent of my own psychology, like Sylvia Barrett
and Paul Barringer, I bumbled through those years. It was
one thing to doubt one's ability to teach effectively; it was
quite another to doubt one's ability to conduct oneself in
a socially appropriate manner. Suddenly, ways of relating
to people—especially males—that had proved effective
throughout my life had become of questionable utility in
the classroom, and were possibly even dangerous or wrong.
What did one do with one's feelings everyday between 8
A.M. and 3 P.M.? How could the person who graded
student papers ever hope to be liked, let alone loved, by
the authors of these documents? What *should* one wear?
Was it bad to be attractive or to joke with the students?
How should one respond to students with crushes? To the
actions of hostile ones? Would administrative authority
figures always trigger the dark side of my childhood
recollections? I found myself feeling my way through a
peculiar and unforseen limbo somewhere between my own
adolescence and adulthood; I thought I knew who I had
been, but I had no idea who I was becoming or how to
speed the transition.

Double Negative

While *Up the Down Staircase* was, for the most part, a
timely and useful book for me, I recall having a few
differences with it. For example, at the very beginning,
when Barrett meets her homeroom group in what is
otherwise an engaging and amusing scene, she asks the

students to fill in address cards. When one boy tells her that he doesn't know his address because his family is moving, she inquires where they are moving and, again, finds he doesn't know. She next asks him where he lives now, and he replies, "I don't live no place" (Kaufman, 1964, p. 16). Automatically, she corrects, "*Any* place," and goes on to talk with another student.

In this episode, Barrett entraps herself in the tangled spider's web of class, language, identity, and pedagogy, which English teachers must evade or reweave. As the daughter of an elementary school teacher who publicly amputated the prepositions at the ends of my sentences and added *m*'s to my *who*'s with the relentless precision of a metronome, I have always prickled with resentment at those who correct the grammar of others in conversation. Perhaps it is this penchant for pedantry that caused a reviewer for *Time Magazine* to describe Sylvia Barrett as "Our Miss Brooks in the Blackboard Jungle."

The other problem I recall having had with the book lay in the character of Dr. Bester, the head of the English Department. Schacter endorses his knowledge of teaching and admonishes Barrett to heed any advice he may give her. A student writes favorably of him, saying that "everyone saw the good teacher shining through the false window of sternness" and adds, "We all worked our head off for him" (Kaufman, 1964, pp. 84-85). Barrett herself admires him for his "masterly handling" of a situation in which, while he is supervising a study hall, a boy tells him to "Go jump in the lake" (1964, p. 77). Bester responds by having the young man repeat each word of the offending phrase several times, rendering the insult ridiculous. Then, having bested the boy in the power struggle, Bester leaves the room. Turning, he adds, "with impeccable courtesy, 'I'll be glad to recommend you for a remedial speech class'" (p. 77).

One of my major problems as a new, young teacher was learning to avoid using use sarcasm to humiliate troublesome and, often, troubled students; I realized that in the classroom, in my role as a teacher, I had power to do serious damage. Whenever I did succumb to the temptation to be sarcastic and let fly a deft and barbed insult, I heard old Mrs. Goodwin's voice intoning, "Now remember, there's no such thing as a bad child." Clearly, Dr. Bester had never conversed with her.

But these niggling criticisms did not detract from the enormous pleasure I took in Kaufman's book. In fact, when I remember reading *Up the Down Staircase* for the first time, I am reminded of a recent reading experience I had after a visit to the Orkney Islands off the north coast of Scotland. I had packed a guidebook describing the area, but somehow, when we arrived on Orkney, we could not locate it. We made do with suggestions from our innkeeper and brochures from the tourist information center for the few days we were there, wandering amazed among ruins of prehistoric fortifications and ancient rings of standing stones. Later, as we cleaned out our much lived-in rented car at the airport at Glasgow, I rummaged under the seat and found, among other things, the missing guidebook. On the plane home, I read about where I had been and what I had seen, nodding and smiling in recognition, just as I had nodded and laughed my way through Kaufman's story of a new teacher in an urban high school.

UP THE DOWN STAIRCASE REVISITED

An article entitled "Sex, Power, and Pedagogy," by British feminist Valerie Walkerdine (1981), illuminates my retrospective reading of *Up the Down Staircase*, particularly with respect to the troubling transactions between teachers and students of opposite gender which drive part of this novel. Walkerdine says, "Relations of power are not invested in unitary individuals in any way which is solely or essentially derived from their material and institutional position" (1981, p. 16). She adds, "The gender and ages of the participants clearly have major effects which serve to displace other variables." While her article discusses young children and not adolescents, I think her arguments are useful in understanding the relationship between female teachers and male students at both Calvin Coolidge and Smithfield High Schools.

One of Walkerdine's points is that a teacher's power can be altered depending on whether her role in a given discourse is that of subject or object. For example, when Joe Ferone looms over Sylvia Barrett in a deserted classroom, he becomes the aggressor, and both his verbal and nonverbal communications to her are fraught with power and menace. Barrett has gone from her institutional role of authoritative, oppressive teacher to one of cowering sex object. Only by assuming a yet more commanding personal role, that of a mother who can reach out and caress away a child's pain, does Barrett overturn the power dynamic between the two, reducing the briefly mighty Ferone to flight and, perhaps, tears. That she was able to do this is a sign of her professional growth and personal maturity as well as a reminder that in fiction, anything is possible.

In the novel, Barrett is working her way toward the attainment of Erikson's "generativity" and Ashton-Warner's "still centre," while back in room A301 at Smithfield, I was still trying to get that year's incarnation of Thomas Abruzzi to stop interrupting and change his seat without hurting his feelings or triggering his misogynistic hostility. Another perspective on the seesaw of seduction and nurturance on which, like Sylvia Barrett, I teetered as a young teacher is that of Grumet (1988), who writes: "The cult of maternal nurturance ignored female sexuality, oblivious to the erotic gratifications of maternity and the sensual and sexual life of the young women it kept under constant surveillance. The teacher was supposed to

banish sensuality from the classroom and her life"
(p. 53). Grumet believes that while celebrating the
"maternal gifts" of the teacher, the patriarchally planned
and run school system has alienated her from her own
feelings, bodies, memories, and dreams, as well as the
sisterhood of other women who are, in fact, the mothers of
her students (1988, p. 57). No wonder Smithfield often
seemed like a convent or prison to the young woman in
the pink, pleated chemise dress teaching in room A301.

Still another perspective that enriched my retrospective
reading of Kaufman's book is David Mamet's play *Ole-
anna*. This riveting and controversial drama takes place
during three conferences between a female college freshman and her education professor. It is a matter of individual interpretation whether the professor has sexually
harassed the student or whether she has deliberately
sabotaged his career. Has there been an abuse of power?
Where, in this context, do the power and the responsibility really lie? Can one decontextualize a particular
transaction from the chain of others that comprise a
relationship? This *Rashomon*-like theatrical experience
reminded me of, among other things, the climactic scenes
between Barrett and Ferone and between Alice Baker and
Paul Barringer. In all three, the potential for violence
and destruction, both physical and psychic, charges the
atmosphere.

I am impressed anew by Kaufman's almost prescient
familiarity with the mined terrain of educational politics,
and with those of us, of both genders, who travel (now
more warily than in 1964) across it. It is noteworthy that
both Kaufman and Ashton-Warner, two seasoned female
teachers publishing in the 1960s, defuse the mines with
the creative force of generative love and "espousal"
respectively. On the other hand, David Mamet, a male
playwright of the 1990s, has not defused the mines at all.
Should he write a script for a theatrical production of
Up the Down Staircase, it would no doubt end in a court-

room, not a classroom.

My recent reading of *Up the Down Staircase* also recalled to me those students whose writings enliven its pages and who, like Ashton-Warner's Maori pupils, demand attention and affection from even the most cynical reader. Their excuses for not turning in homework ("My dog pead on it"; p. 165), their notes in the suggestion box ("I'm getting behine because school goes to fast for me to retain the work. Maybe if they go more slower with the readings? Repeter"; p. 186), and their get-well messages to Barrett when she is hospitalized with a broken foot ("I complaned a lot. but I didn't know how lucky I was to have you. until we got this jerky sub. she don't know a thing and she's trying to teach it. Miguel Rios"; p. 332) are wrenching.

Suddenly, I found myself waxing nostalgic about my years at Smithfield for the first time since I began reflecting on my experiences there for this project. Rereading the messages of Calvin Coolidge's students was like looking at photos from a trip to Mexico. By the time the pictures have been developed and retrieved from the shop, recollections of crippling dysentery, third-degree sunburn, and near-fatal insect bites have paled beside the more vivid memories of pristine beaches, charming villages, and archeological miracles.

4

To Sir, with Love:
E. R. Braithwaite

A RETROSPECTIVE RESPONSE

Reading *To Sir, with Love* by E. R. Braithwaite was much like buying sunglasses when I paid a February visit to my daughter who was studying in Arizona. I had not remembered to bring any, so on the drive from the Tucson airport, the glaring desert light nearly blinded me. The very first thing I did after checking into my hotel was buy a pair. Only then could I appreciate the striking saguaro-strewn landscape which was rimmed by mountains. In just the same fashion, after reading Braithwaite's book, I could better see where I was going on my expedition through the murk of institutionalized racism that had partly colored my own education and was clouding that of my students.

When I read *To Sir, with Love* in 1965, it was the first book I had ever read by a person of color. A friend who had listened to me rhapsodizing over *Up the Down Stair-case* suggested it as another good book about a teacher, so I checked it out of the Westville branch of the New Haven Public Library and quickly devoured it. Published in England in 1959 and in the United States in 1960, *To*

Sir, with Love existed in print for a long time before the film was released. I, for one, am grateful, because for me, Braithwaite's story was extremely useful.

In his autobiographical book, Braithwaite explains how he finds himself, a trained and experienced communications engineer in the petroleum industry, teaching in a high school in London's impoverished East End. Although Braithwaite was born and raised in British Guiana (now Guyana), according to Jani Prescott in *Contemporary Author New Revision Series* (1989), he graduated from City University of New York in 1940 with a Bachelor of Science degree (p. 40). After working for two years as communications engineer for the Standard Oil Company at their Aruba Refinery, he earned enough money to pay for postgraduate work in England at Cambridge University (Braithwaite, 1959, p. 37). During World War II, he served for six years as a Royal Air Force fighter pilot. While in the service, Braithwaite had made a point of keeping up with new developments in electronics by borrowing books through the Central Library System and subscribing to technical journals and magazines. Assorted career counselors who met with him in the course of the demobilization of the British forces in 1945 were extremely encouraging about his prospects for finding employment in light of his experience and education, as well as because of the expected boom in postwar production (Braithwaite, 1959, p. 37).

Then, Braithwaite recounts his shock, humiliation, sadness, and anger at the rejections that inevitably followed when potential employers learned that he was black. He describes the aftermath of one particular encounter:

I felt drained of strength and thought; yet somehow I managed to leave that office, navigate that passage, lift and corridor, and walk out of the building into the busy sunlit street. I had just been brought face to face with something I had either forgotten or completely ignored for more than six exciting years—my black skin. It had not mattered when I volunteered for aircrew service in 1940, it had not mattered during the period of flying training or when I received my wings and was posted to a squadron; it had not mattered in the hectic uncertainties of operational flying, of living and loving from day to day, brothered to men who like myself had no tomorrow and could not afford to fritter away today on the absurdities of prejudice; it had not mattered when, uniformed and winged, I visited theatres, dance-halls, pubs, and private houses. (1959, p. 39)

Braithwaite spent nearly eighteen frustrating and disheartening months looking for work in postwar London, to no avail. He was "overpigmented" for the engineering-management jobs for which his training and experience qualified him, and overqualified for the service jobs for which he stood a chance of being considered. During this period, he reflects on the many guises of racism in Britain, the British colonies, and America. He gives in to a "poisoning hatred," which is relieved by occasional acts of friendliness and unselfishness on the part of others. For example, sitting in St. James Park one day, he allows himself to be drawn into conversation by an elderly gentleman whom he has seen there often. Noting the young man's dejection, this philosophical stranger uses war imagery to describe city life saying, "A great city is a battlefield. . . . You need to be a fighter to live in it, not exist, mark you, live" (Braithwaite, 1959, p. 48).

Upon hearing Braithwaite's story, this new advisor suggests he get a teaching job. When Braithwaite protests that he lacks training as a teacher, the older man responds: "Oh that's not absolutely necessary. Your degrees would be considered in lieu of training, and I feel sure that with your experience and obvious ability you could do well" (Braithwaite, 1959, p. 48). At this point in their dialogue, Braithwaite poses a key question: "Look here, Sir, if these people would not let me near ordinary inanimate objects about which I understand quite a bit, is it reasonable to expect them to entrust the education of their children to me?" (p. 48). After considerable discussion, the stranger

convinces Braithwaite to apply for a job teaching in
London's East End where, since it is a poor and tough
area, there are, of course, many vacancies, and Braithwaite's race is not likely to be an issue.

Braithwaite's story and his reflections on it forced me
to confront my own racism, that of my friends and family,
and that which I was finding built into the tracking system
at Smithfield. By the time I encountered the book,
America had begun to turn inside out around this issue.
Thus, my personal reaction to Braithwaite's narrative
paralleled a national awakening, being thus greatly inten-
sified. Braithwaite contrasts British prejudice with what
he had seen in America where, he says, "When prejudice
is felt, it is open, obvious, blatant; the white man makes
his position very clear, and the black man fights those
prejudices with equal openness and fervour, using every
constitutional device available to him" (1959, p. 43).
Understandably, my perception of the impact of prejudice in America differed from Braithwaite's since it was
woven from the strands of my own personal history.

My childhood had for a time included an African-
American domestic worker named Bessie Bridges, who
came to our home from Newark every weekday to cook
and clean. She was stout and spirited, a warm, smiling
presence, who was ever in motion and seemingly content.
I remember when I asked my mother what the long,
crescent-shaped welt on Bessie's arm was and she told
me that Bessie's friend Leroy had stabbed her, leaving a
scar. After that, Bessie seemed mysterious, and it occurred to me that each day when she left our house to take
the bus back to Newark, Bessie resumed a life that was
private and somehow profoundly different from the rather
humdrum routines of our household. Although my parents
liked Bessie and appreciated her work, they referred to her
in conversation with others as "the girl" and made it very
clear that she was separate from us, even as she was in our
midst. Although I sensed the ambiguity of Bessie's role

in our domestic life, as a child I could not articulate it. It seemed part of the natural order of things in the world I knew, where people who had household help were white and their helpers were Negro.

As I have mentioned in this narrative, my school experiences did nothing to challenge the racial prejudices that I had absorbed from my family. In fact, these prejudices were reinforced by school. Reading *To Sir, with Love*, I recalled how few people of color had been in my college preparatory classes in high school or my classes at Vassar. By 1965 I understood that the tracking-testing systems at Jersey and Smithfield high schools had been quietly and routinely perpetuating the segregation of most African-Americans into general and vocational rather than college preparatory classes. As a result, all through school, I had been segregated from African-Americans and had simply assumed that most of them were not smart enough to go to college because they were not in the same classes as I; as a high school student in the 1950s, I had not thought much about race, and as a college student, I had thought about it even less.

Given these facts of my life, before I came to Smithfield I might have shared Braithwaite's perception that black people in America were protected from the impact of prejudice by the Constitution, but my few years at Smithfield had disabused me of that notion. Smithfield's rigid tracking system left little opportunity for students of different races and social classes to mingle; membership in the upper-level college preparatory sections helped ensure good recommendations to good colleges, while membership in the General Education sections more or less ruled out the possibility of going to college at all. And there was no mistaking the class and color of the great majority of the college preparatory students or, for that matter, the lower class and darker color of the great majority of those who had not "chosen" to attend college.

I knew now that our American rhetoric was democratic

but that for many citizens, the reality was not; it was the same reality that Braithwaite encounters as he tries to find work and later tries to teach in London. The British way of life which he had been schooled to respect and love as a boy and for which he had risked his life as a man, has proven to be a sham, and Braithwaite must struggle not only to find employment but, like me, to reconstruct his world and his identity (1959, p. 44).

Black Like Him

Black, British, and male, E. R. Braithwaite was in some ways an unlikely role model for me, but in other ways he provided a fine example, for in *To Sir, with Love* he is constantly examining and reexamining his philosophy, pedagogy, and personality as he struggles to transform himself from an embittered, out-of-work engineer to Sir, the beloved teacher of forty-six students at Greenslade Secondary School. As I have indicated, I needed to do some transforming of my own, and he was helpful in mentoring me through my metamorphosis.

Like me, Braithwaite is incontrovertibly middle-class, committed to working his way through an orderly, cultured, and civilized life. I had met very few educated people of color during my youth, and I had known none well. At Smithfield, I made my first African-American friend: Beverly, a slightly older woman who also taught English. We bonded for life one day in a fit of conspiratorial giggles over the affected and pompous way in which Mr. Schwartzman dragged out the pronunciation of her name. However, I recall with embarrassment asking Beverly if blacks got sunburned, curious in much the same way Braithwaite's students are when they ask him questions about the color of his blood. I also recall being surprised by the fact that Beverly spoke Standard English with no southern accent or dialect and owned a home in a comfortable suburb. I was similarly surprised by Braithwaite's British prose, proper manners, and affinity for ballet, theater, and classical music. Through his book, he became my second black friend.

In *To Sir, with Love* Braithwaite chronicles the evolution of a teacher starting with his first days in the classroom, when he uses sarcasm, oral reading, and written work to assess and control the rebellious white, working-class adolescents he finds there. Dissatisfied with his performance during his early weeks at Greenslade, he then studies his students, exploring their impoverished neighborhood and observing them at recess and in assembly. He sifts through the assorted bits of advice he gets from his new colleagues, discusses his problems with his kindly landlord and landlady, and seeks suggestions as well as support from the Head, A. Florian. He obtains and reads books on the psychology of teaching, of which he says: "The suggested methods somehow did not meet my particular need, and just did not work. It was as if I were trying to reach the children through a thick pane of glass" (1959, p. 67). He spends hours on his plans, trying to frame the subjects he teaches in the context of the students' own lives, both present and future. Still, he meets that resistance so familiar to the neophyte teacher, first silence and passivity, then noise and more activity, and finally, openly hostile confrontation to his authority, followed swiftly in Braithwaite's case by muttered racial insults as students congratulate one another for "putting the black bastard in his place" (1959, p. 69).

As Braithwaite taps futilely on the pane of glass separating him from his students, he grows increasingly concerned, not only about their disrespectful treatment of him, but also about their disrespect toward one another. He is troubled by their rough, discourteous language, slovenly and tasteless dress, and casually bawdy banter and behavior. When, one day after lunch, a used sanitary napkin is found burning in the fireplace grate in the classroom, Braithwaite is overcome by anger and disgust. He loses his temper and, banishing the boys from the room, gives the girls an old-fashioned tongue lashing in which he includes feedback about "their general conduct, rude language, sluttish behaviour and . . . free and easy familiarity with the boys" (1959, p. 71).

This episode proves a turning point for Braithwaite, and the next day, he lays out a credo which he shapes more or less "at the point of utterance." He announces to his students his desire to share his plans with all of them, to be reasonable, to listen without interrupting, and to try to be interesting as well as relevant. He indicates also his receptivity to questions and feedback and his intention to treat them as young men and women who, as seniors, set the standards of conduct and achievement for the rest of the school (1959, pp. 73-77).

In this manifesto, Braithwaite requires the boys to address the girls as "Miss So and So" and the girls to address the boys by their surnames. He himself is to be called "Sir" by everyone. Braithwaite begins his reform, not with academic matters, but with attention to the interpersonal climate in which he and students will work together. He indicates his willingness to help them alter their social code to one that is better suited to their school life as well as to the work world they are preparing to enter. His classroom research has revealed to him the "centers of leadership" and he exploits these in order to change the culture of their learning community (1959, p. 76).

How I envied the facility with which Braithwaite almost magically transforms his class from a group of ill-mannered, recalcitrant teens to mature models of self-respect and mutual consideration. I wished that my lectures met with similar results, and I had to keep reminding myself that Braithwaite was older, a military hero and man of the world, while I was young, female, and singularly lacking in worldly experience. When my envy threatened to overwhelm me, I went so far as to remind myself that Braithwaite was, after all, a character in his own book and so could telescope events in time, while I, on the other hand, was trapped in the reality of Smithfield, and therefore had to serve a considerably longer apprenticeship.

And during this apprenticeship, an ongoing problem for me was how to deal with behavior that on the surface was rude and personal but that was really an expression of anger at forces that reached far beyond the confines of room A301. I remember a sophomore General English class in the spring of 1964, during which Laverne Watson damned me several times. I took her to Miss Nolan, English Department Head, who saw fit to intercede by saying: "Laverne, did you see Mrs. Kennedy on television? Do you remember how straight and proudly she stood at that funeral? What a lady she was? How she remained silent and stoic no matter how she felt? Well, don't you think you could be like that in school?" There followed an unforgettable moment or two when Miss Nolan, now fully into her Pygmalion mode, began bending Laverne's arms at the elbows and folding Laverne's hands at her waist. I stood open-mouthed, expecting Miss Nolan to pull a pillbox hat out of her sleeve and bobby pin it to Laverne's pageboy.

Laverne, a statuesque and feisty African-American teenager, became mannequinlike in her submission to this manipulation. As we left the office, she cursed me anew, albeit this time under her breath. But I no longer blamed her, even though I could not have articulated then what had been so terribly wrong with the tableau Miss Nolan had been trying to create. It seemed a bizarre response to Laverne, her behavior, and our shared setting at Smithfield, and it was a long time before I again availed myself of Miss Nolan's intervention. Just as I blamed some of my failures on forces outside the confines of room A301, I had to attribute some of Braithwaite's success to the nature of the administration of Greenslade Secondary School.

Whole School, Whole Teacher, Whole Child

A. Florian, the Head at Greenslade, is a progressive educator who, "consider[s] himself merely one of a team engaged in important and necessary work; he [is] spokesman and official representative of the team, but [seeks] no personal aggrandisement because of that" (1959, p. 13). At their initial meeting, he tells Braithwaite, "Things are done here somewhat differently from the usual run, and many teachers have found it, shall we say, disquieting" (1959, p. 14). After Braithwaite has had a chance to observe a few classes and an assembly and to meet his potential colleagues, he decides to accept the position being offered. Then, Florian details for Braithwaite the attitudes toward the children, the community, and the educational process that shape policy and practice at Greenslade.

Before coming to Greenslade, the students have all "shown some disregard for, or opposition to, authority"; in Florian's view, this authority depended on fear, "either of the stick or some other form of punishment." At Greenslade, the students are viewed as "men and women in the process of development," and Florian does not allow that development to be "forced or restricted at the arbitrary whim of any individual who by some accident of fortune is in a position to exercise some authority over them" (1959, p. 30).

Florian goes on to explain that the students live amid the myriad pressures of poverty, which the school staff is obliged to try to understand so as to best help them. He adds that Greenslade's faculty tries to improve the poor conduct of their students by "affection, confidence, and guidance, more or less in that order." He wants

each student to "work, play, and express himself without
fear."   Florian envisions Greenslade as a force in the
children's lives that must "outweigh" the evil around
them.   His final words to Braithwaite are, "Remember,
they're wonderful children when you get to know them"
(1959, p. 31).

This man is clearly Mrs. Goodwin's British counterpart.
Short, with "eyes dancing like those of a mischievous
imp," Florian even shares Mrs. Goodwin's elfin appearance
(1959, p. 14).   Braithwaite is not sure that Florian is
serious when he speaks of the students "as if they [a]re all
tiny helpless children, a description very much at vari-
ance with the husky youths and girls jiving in the auditorium" (1959, p. 32).   Florian offers Braithwaite his
support and help, as well as that of his staff.

One of the practices that Florian has institutionalized at
Greenslade is the Weekly Review.   "Each child review[s]
the events of his school week in his own words, in his own
way; he [i]s free to comment, to criticize, to agree or
disagree with any person, subject, or method as long as it
[i]s in some way associated with the school" (1959, p. 66).
This is a pet scheme of the Head, designed to help students improve their written expression, provide feedback
for the teachers, and aid in planning.

Not surprisingly, Florian's attitudes are mirrored by
most teachers, and only one or two disparage the students.
The rest of Braithwaite's colleagues respect them and try
to help them and each other in many ways.   When Braithwaite proposes taking all forty-six of his charges on a
field trip, Florian releases another teacher to accompany
the group.   Other colleagues assist Braithwaite by sharing
their advice and welcoming him into their classrooms to
observe their own work.   At Braithwaite's request, the
domestic science teacher speaks to the students about
hygiene and grooming.

Florian has also institutionalized an improved version of
the daily assembly at Greenslade in which the students

eagerly attend and thoroughly enjoy a schoolwide program of poetry and classical music that begins with a non-denominational prayer and takes place against a colorful backdrop created by the art classes. It is at such a gathering that Florian introduces Braithwaite to Green-slade's student body.

In this supportive and nurturing setting, it is easy to accept Braithwaite's accomplishments. Unlike those of us at Smithfield, he did not have to cope with the inane policies and grandiose rhetoric of Mr. Schwartzman or the obsessive demands of Miss Nolan. Like his students, he is free to work and express himself without fear. He can ponder the feedback in the Weekly Reviews, use the assemblies to publicly reward students for work well done, and reach out for help, confident he will get a genuinely helpful response from colleagues and the Head. Even the fact that Greenslade lacks central heating and indoor plumbing does not detract from its desirability as a teaching and learning environment.

However, I questioned a statement Florian makes early on to Braithwaite: "As things are, we cannot expect of them high academic effort, but we can take steps to in-sure that their limited abilities are exploited to the full" (1959, p. 32). I understood that the lives of the Green-slade students were not designed to facilitate book learn-ing, but I no longer accepted the fact that this should automatically equate with "limited ability." I attributed this discrepancy between my opinion and Florian's to the notorious British class system (Holbrook, 1964) until I really began to look at the assumptions about race and class underlying our own educational tracking and sorting.

This system had created one especially memorable group that I taught that consisted of nine remedial readers, all male and all African-American. They were juniors, but reportedly read way below grade. An exhaustive search of the book closet yielded only one, *The Glass Menagerie*, that seemed even remotely appropriate for my spirited students. Daily we formed our circle and enacted the play, with all of us taking turns with all of the roles, regardless of gender. We also took time out for discussions that were remarkably candid and wide ranging. One issue that emerged had to do with what we used to call the generation gap; another was the eligibility of various types of people as suitors or "gentlemen callers." Not surprisingly, these topics led us to consider interracial dating and marriage, and I was delighted by the psychological and sociological insight with which these "remedial readers" approached such a complex and controversial subject. They certainly were not remedial thinkers.

In fact, as he gets to know his students better, Braithwaite, too, learns to respect their intelligence, curiosity, and maturity (1959, pp. 80-85). Their discussions cover many disciplines, and Braithwaite shares information about his life, his travels, and his beliefs with them (1959, p. 86). When one of the more rebellious boys stages a boxing match as a kind of last stand, Braithwaite reluctantly decks him, almost as if he understands the boy's need to be forced into a new and more accepting stance. While reading *To Sir, with Love*, I continued to look at my own daily experience from Braithwaite's perspective. In this way, I saw a wider range of possible responses to students as well as a broader context for interaction, for Braithwaite engages with all forty-six people in his class intellectually, emotionally, socially, and physically, with the whole teacher taking on the whole student in an effort to bring about learning and change (1959, p. 85).

One of Braithwaite's major contributions to the young men and women he teaches is social, racial, and political awareness. He shares his personal constructs and values with his students, patiently deconstructing their racist attitudes and biases. The most moving part of his narrative shows the slow progress the students make under his guidance in attempting to integrate their school learning with their home values. Braithwaite divulges to the reader

his own bitterness and pain as the students struggle to
expand their social setting outside school to include people
of color (1959, pp. 170-72).

Among Braithwaite's students is Larry Seales, the son
of a white mother and a West Indian father. The Seales
family has long resided in the neighborhood, where Mrs.
Seales works in the laundry alongside parents of many
of Larry's classmates (1959, p. 169). Mrs. Seales dies
suddenly, and Larry's classmates decide to collect money
with which to purchase flowers for the funeral. However,
they tell Braithwaite that none of them can deliver the
flowers to the Seales home because of "what people would
say if they saw us going into a colored person's home"
(1959, p. 168). Braithwaite is astounded and profoundly
upset by this declaration. Finally, one especially mature
and sensitive girl volunteers to deliver the bouquet.

But the unwillingness of the rest of the class to be seen
in the home of a "colored" person causes Braithwaite to
question his own forthcoming marriage to a white woman,
as well as his year of work with the students. He laments,
"I felt weak and useless, an alien among them. All the
weeks and months of delightful association were washed
out by those few words" (1959, p. 168). For the second
time in this short book, Braithwaite is caught off guard by
the racism that pervades British life at all levels.

However, when he visits the Seales family the next day,
prior to the funeral, he is surprised and moved to find his
students there after all. He describes this scene:

And then I stopped, feeling suddenly washed clean, whole and
alive again. Tears were in my eyes, unashamedly, for there,
standing in a close, separate group on the pavement outside
Seales' door was my class, my children, all or nearly all of them,
smart and selfconscious in their best clothes. Oh God, forgive
me for the hateful thoughts, because I love them, these brutal,
disarming bastards, I love them. (1959, p. 172)

In 1965 my tears mingled with Braithwaite's as I choked

with an unclarified but strong emotion. In reading about this incident, I shared Braithwaite's joy and relief, his renewed faith in the power of love and example.

In effect, Braithwaite's own multicultural persona as a black Guyanan teaching white teenagers in postcolonial England strikes a dissonant chord in the educational system. Braithwaite's dissonance is rendered all the more jarring by virtue of his integrity and self-awareness as he becomes an embodiment of all the issues confronting those who work in multiculutual communities. His very existence in their midst forces the youngsters to reconstrue their world. And he himself must constantly struggle to reassess his own place in their world and the world at large. E. R. Braithwaite was partly responsible for my decision in the summer of 1966 to apply for a grant to study "The Ethnic Writer in Urban America" and "Psychology and Sociology in African-American Literature" at Wesleyan University, which I discuss in chapter 6. It was time to supplement the inadequate baggage I had brought with me on my teaching journey with other material better suited to the climate and terrain I was exploring.

TO SIR, WITH LOVE REVISITED

To Sir, with Love remains a moving and provocative reading experience. I am always impressed anew by Braithwaite's ability to transcend his own bitterness and racism in order to do the job he has undertaken. By contextualizing his teaching practice in a very condensed summary of his preservice life experiences, Braithwaite convinces the reader of his marginality, even as he confronts it himself. In a sense, his politicalization is analogous to that described by Sue Middleton, a New Zealand sociologist of women's education, when interpreting studies of working class women in bourgeois white academic settings. She says:

These analyses suggest that people who develop radical (e.g., feminist) views of the social world have experienced in their lives contradictions and/or a sense of marginality and have access to radical social theories which articulate their private problems as outcomes of structural inequalities in society. The unpleasantness of experiences such as marginality, alienation, or irreconcilable contradictions, makes personal or social change seem desireable. Education helps to make such changes seem possible. (1992, p. 24)

In light of the importance I now attribute to personality and preservice experience in shaping one's teaching praxis, I recognize Braithwaite as an intelligent survivor who had already succeeded in studying and working his way half around the world, and who had also lived to recall six years of active wartime service in the Royal Air Force. Braithwaite's story offers readers an opportunity to reflect on their own personalities and past experiences; no matter how often I reread the passage in which Braithwaite discovers that his students have, after all, gone to the Seales home to pay their respects to their classmate on the death of his mother, I am stirred to tears. Even typing these lines, I find my vision blurring. It occurs to me in retrospect that in 1993, my emotional response to this portion of the text is strong because I identify with Braithwaite, but in 1965, I probably identified to some extent with his students who, like me, had to separate from the racist views of their families of origin in order to grow up. That separation and its attendant pain are part of what my struggle at Smithfield, and throughout the 1960s, involved. That was very likely what my tears were about then, but I didn't realize it until now.

By the book's end, Braithwaite has not only triumphed in the classroom, he has also wooed and won the affection of a young white teacher with whom he had fallen in love. Throughout the story, Braithwaite has made his home with an elderly British couple he met during the war, whom he calls Mom and Dad and who support and nurture him during his tribulations. He defies the stereotype of the engineer with a calculator for a heart; rather, he is a warm person far from home who reaches out for, and receives, familial and romantic love.

I am also impressed by Braithwaite's maturity, which enables him to make decisions that are informed by experience and self-awareness. Well over thirty, he is a highly capable adult learner who teaches himself how to teach. Like that of Sylvia Barrett, Braithwaite's pedagogy is not especially revolutionary, but his personal involvement and investment in the teaching process make it more meaningful than it would have been otherwise. By spending time and energy preparing relevant material, taking students on field trips, and openly explaining his own perspective, Braithwaite imbues his teaching with the caring that Nel Noddings (1984) advocates—caring that makes all the difference. In a sense, he himself becomes part of the curriculum, as his students study him for clues on how to live and learn in a difficult world. *To Sir, with Love* fills the contemporary reader with appreciation, not only for the individual who can open up to scrutiny and involvement, as Braithwaite does, but also for those rare administrators who, like A. Florian, assume responsibility for creating and maintaining an environment in which teachers feel free to experiment, engage, and reflect.

In addition, Braithwaite's story offers readers an opportunity to examine the cross-gender dynamics between teacher and student that I discussed in chapter 3. When an attractive student named Pamela Dare develops a crush on him, Braithwaite manages to defuse her growing interest without hurting her feelings or demeaning her in any way. He is aware of the students' developed sexuality and the tensions it causes; however, he is not in danger of being overwhelmed by it. He simply wants them to relate across gender lines with the same mutual respect he feels should govern all interpersonal transactions.

Braithwaite shows great concern for a boy who is

wrongly accused of a crime and another whose mother has just died. He is paternal in the best sense of the word, a generative and nurturing force who visits the students' homes and families when doing so will prevent or solve a problem. I was saddened by newspaper stories of the accidental shooting of Brooklyn elementary school principal Pat Daley in the winter of 1992. According to all reports, he, too, was a caring, nurturing man who worked with students in an impoverished and crime-infested neighborhood. When I read accounts of how he used to escort youngsters home to be sure they were safe and how beloved he was, I think at once of E. R. Braithwaite.

To Sir, with Love has much to say to those among us who live in a world still divided into warring tribes. In much autobiographical literature by people of color there is an attempt to show how the author relates to inhabitants of the white world, the world of the oppressors. However, it is noteworthy that Braithwaite, a black Guyanan in postcolonial England, finds himself entrusted with "the education of their children" and transcends his own rage and bitterness to educate his charges with wisdom, respect, and love. I am glad I read *To Sir, with Love* when I did, for it prepared me for the next valuable guidebook on which I happened.

5

How Children Fail: John Holt

A RETROSPECTIVE RESPONSE

Although it was easy for me to identify with E. R. Braith-waite, Sylvia Barrett, and Sylvia Ashton-Warner, I had a hard time identifying with John Holt when I read *How Children Fail* early in my teaching journey. In this book, Holt records in diary form his observations in a colleague's fifth grade classroom at the private Colorado Rocky Mountain School as well as experiences from his own teaching. His account focuses on student behavior and includes meticulously reported details of "strategies" that pupils use to protect themselves from losing face, being wrong, changing approaches, and, in short, from learning. Rather than identifying with the author, I identified with the middle school students he describes, for I recognized and remembered using all the strategies they employ.

Another reason I didn't identify with Holt was that in the throes of my own crowded classes and demanding schedule at Smithfield, I couldn't imagine recording the minutiae of student behavior as he had done. At the time I thought it was weird that he had logged with such painstaking specificity the goings on in his classroom. To keep a teaching journal at Smithfield, I felt, would have been like writing in one's travelogue from a raft while careening down the rapids of the Colorado River.

A further reason for my nonidentification with Holt was that I found his straightforward account austere; there is no humor, little personality, and even less romance. Even though the situation he recounts is tragic, I, who weep copiously during New York Telephone's "We're All Connected" commercials, shed nary a tear when I read *How Children Fail.* Sylvia Ashton-Warner's classroom journals are, in contrast, so impassioned, personal, and exotic that they have always seemed an effortless and inevitable outpouring, like lines she couldn't help writing sitting by the fire in the evening.

So why do I include John Holt in the roster of those whose writing illuminated my path as a young teacher? I include him because he did, in fact, enable me to reconnect with the student I had once been at a time when I was in danger of believing that I had more or less learned how to teach. By that, I mean that by 1965, I had mastered the rudiments of what is now referred to as "classroom management"; in other words, the overtly hostile student was the exception rather than the rule, and since the students viewed me as the lesser among the available evils, I was actually popular with many. In view of my increasing usefulness, even the administration regarded me favorably—so favorably, in fact, that my request to transfer to a new and reportedly progressive high school opening in downtown New Haven in 1966 was denied because, as Mr. Schwartzman drawled: "You're one of our best teachers. We don't want to lose you." I was in real danger of fitting in at Smithfield when John Holt rescued me from professional complacency, which is the enemy of professional growth and competence. He didn't make me cry, but he did make me think.

Holt is adamant that we teachers ourselves are responsible for the sense of our methods and deplores blaming students for their failure to learn. And he points out that even students who seem successful employ strategies aimed at disguising the fact that they, too, have not learned, in spite of their high grades and apparent mastery. There is Walter, a seemingly able student with good marks and a reputation as "brilliant." Holt transcribes the dialogue between himself and Walter as the latter attempts to figure out, "If you are travelling at 40 miles per hour, how long will it take you to go 10 miles?" Holt deconstructs the child's efforts into two strategies: "numeral shoving," the manipulation of numbers which enables Walter to come up with the "right answer," and "word shoving," the manipulation of words which enables him to come up with a reasonable sounding explanation of how he got this answer. Unfortunately, Walter's subsequent conversation reveals that he does not understand the problem, let alone the solution (Holt, 1964/1982, pp. 29-31).

The first section of *How Children Fail* is devoted to describing and illustrating the assorted strategies that Holt catalogues. In addition to numeral and word shoving, there are mumbling the answer in the hope that the teacher will assume it is correct; raising your hand assertively, knowing that the teacher is prone to call on those who seem uncertain; and hedging so that if you have the wrong answer, it seems as if you knew it was wrong and are not, therefore, really stupid. Furthermore, Holt depicts the precision, born of desperation, with which the children have learned to read the teacher's gestures, facial expressions, and stance at the board for clues to the desired response.

Holt concludes, "What goes on in class is not what teachers think—certainly not what I had always thought" (1982, p. 32). He advocates the long observation of students, not just when they are called on to perform, but also during the discussion and explication time when something is ostensibly being "taught." It is during these times that he finds them daydreaming, passing notes, whispering, and doodling. He compares the teacher in class to "a man in the woods at night with a powerful flashlight in his hand. Wherever he turns his light, the creatures on whom it shines are aware of it, and do not behave as they do in the dark" (1982, p. 33).

Holt claims that teachers are more interested in manipulating and controlling students than in understanding them (1982, p. 34). It is his willingness to blame teachers for much of the stress, and the attendant failure that children experience in school, that commanded my attention back at Smithfield. And once he had gotten my attention, Holt inspired in me a clumsy sort of reflection on my own practice. Just as Braithwaite had moved me to recognize and acknowledge my own racism, so Holt drove me to consider the price I had, perhaps, paid for control. Were my students afraid of me?

The Dragon Lady Meets the Diarist

Holt places the blame for the fear that cripples would-be learners on teachers when he comments on Andy, a particularly troubled and troublesome student, by saying: "It is no accident that this boy is afraid. We have made him afraid, consciously, deliberately, so that we might more easily control his behavior and get him to do whatever we wanted him to do" (1982, p. 126). Holt goes on to confess his horror at his own use of fear and anxiety as "instruments of control" in order to get the work done. He notes, "The freedom from fear that I try to give with one hand I almost instantly take away with the other" (1982, p. 127). Later, Holt adds that teachers want children who are "just enough afraid of us to do everything we want, without making us feel that fear of us is what is making them do it" (1982, p. 274).

In 1965 at Smithfield, my students had two nicknames for me. One was "Miz I," a convenient contraction of my long name. I thought it was informal, and perhaps even slightly affectionate, or at least familiar, and I liked it. My other nickname was "Puff." At first, I thought this tag was a reference to my hair which, during the course of my "professionalization," I had reorganized from a ponytail into a severe, bun-type arrangement atop my head. No doubt this topknot had something to do with my second nickname, but one day, when my group of remedial reading students had returned from the lunch break that fragmented our class, they were all humming the tune to "Puff the Magic Dragon," a popular song of the early 1960s. Then I understood: I was a sort of magic dragon lady to them, one minute a frolicsome and lovable denizen of the mythical and misty land of Honahlee, and the next, a powerful and potentially dangerous creature capable of disposing of pirate ships with a single "fearless roar." By dubbing me "Puff," my students indicated their sensitivity to the conflicted and paradoxical nature of my relationship with them, as I, like Holt, rationed out freedom with one hand, only to recall it, seemingly at whim, with the other. If my students were afraid of me, and I am sure that some of them were, it was comforting to know that Holt shared my dilemma.

In the second section of his book, called "Fear and Failure," Holt elaborates on the lengths to which children will go to avoid appearing stupid in the classroom, or on the athletic field. He is as relentless a chronicler outside the school as he is within it, and so no place or situation escapes his mindful eye and patient pen. In one instance, he observes a youngster who appears retarded and her mother in the audience of a children's concert and marvels at the girl's obsessive attention to an ice cream cone that she is studiously eating. He is struck by the "ghastly expression" on the girl's face as she casts furtive glances at her mother to make sure "what she was doing was alright" (1982, p. 97). After a considerable discussion of what it must be like to be retarded and, hence, often incapable of spontaneous, age-appropriate behavior, Holt asks:

If adult intolerance of behavior that to these kids seems natural makes terrified monsters out of what began as merely slow children, what are we to do? We have to draw some line between behavior approved and behavior disapproved, or how is the child to learn? But the great difference between the normal child and the retarded child is that the former is punished for his "bad" behavior; the latter may not be punished, but he is abhorred, which is far worse. (1982, p. 105)

In his effort to drive home the point that "sickening anxiety" about adult responses compels some children's behavior, he is quick to note that in the culture of delinquents, some of whom he encounters on Boston Common, "their ability to shock and horrify is a kind of power over other people" (1982, p. 106). He analyzes gang members as "no more than uneasy allies, welded together partly by fear of the world outside and partly by the certain knowledge that nobody else in the world gives a damn about them" (1982, p. 107).

Holt recounts an episode from one of his own flute lessons when, after a particularly bad day at school, he is intimidated by his music teacher's desire for him to play a particular piece faster than he is prepared to do. He experiences a phenomenon he calls "noteblindness" when, in reaction to a sense of pressure building both in and on his head, he sees the notes but cannot read them. As they seem to move about on the page, they become totally alien to him and his previous experience. His teacher, realizing from the silence that something is amiss, authorizes a short break, and when Holt does resume playing, it is at a slower pace. Holt speculates on what an experience like this, which was both frightening and unpleasant, might mean to a child (1982, p. 118). "Suppose I had not been free, or felt free, to turn away? Suppose my teacher had felt that it would be good for my character to force the pace harder than ever?"

As I mentioned earlier, Holt compelled me into a reunion with the little girl I had been: not the child who read early and easily, but the one who could never understand how many miles per hour anybody went or how long it took her; the one whom her third grade music teacher made sing from behind the piano so no one would hear the dissonant noises she made; the one who crumpled up her blotched and botched attempts at artwork before they could be judged; and the very same one who repeated kindergarten because she couldn't learn to skip. It was in *How Children Fail* that I first gained some conscious understanding of my own early defenses against adult disapproval. It was validating to learn, not only what I had been doing as a child, but why I had done it and, most important, that many other children had also used similar protective strategies in school. Thus, I welcomed my math-phobic, atonal, visually illiterate, and physically uncoordinated former self along on my teaching odyssey as a conscience. She would help me to ignore the siren song of complacency.

To Think, Perchance to Learn . . .

Holt's emphasis on the dangers of the fear of failure is, of course, linked to his notion of what it takes to learn, or succeed. He argues: "Success should not be quick or easy, and should not come all the time. Success implies overcoming an obstacle, including, perhaps, the thought in our minds that we might not succeed. It is turning 'I can't' into 'I can, and I did'" (1982, p. 67). Holt believes that we should lead children to expect a certain amount of failure, which is not in itself a bad thing. In fact, today's failure or mistake may lead to tomorrow's success. Holt asks his students directly, "What do you think, what goes through your mind, when the teacher asks you a question and you don't know the answer?" (1982, p. 71). In response, his students clamor to acknowledge their fear, and Holt reports that he is

flabbergasted—to find this in a school which people think of as progressive; which does its best not to put pressure on little children; which does not give marks in the lower grades; which tries to keep children from feeling that they're in some kind of race. Even in the kindest and gentlest of schools, children are afraid, many of them a great deal of the time, some of them almost all of the time. (1982, p. 71)

Holt's question makes the children's fear explicit and discussable and, Holt believes, "One way to keep down tension is to be aware of it" (1982, p. 76). In an effort to give the children an opportunity and the words for articulating their confusion—to legitimize it—he uses a non-academic analogy, which he calls "foolish" but which actually proves wise indeed. He tells them that to let something go by without knowing what it means and without asking is "like leaving something in Howard Johnson's on a long car trip. You are going to have to go back for it eventually, so the sooner the better." Gratefully, the children learn to recognize the onset of panic and confusion and say, "I'm getting left at Howard Johnson's," making it easier for Holt to retrieve them (1982, p. 76).

Holt's effort to alleviate the fear that cripples children is connected to his view of intelligence. He sees intelligent children as "intensely involved with life," acting "as if they thought the universe made some sense" and "the universe can be trusted," and very different from those fearful youngsters who grab desperately for quick answers in an effort to ease the unbearable tension they feel when they don't know something (1982, p. 89). Toleration of uncertainty is a necessary part of the personality of the intelligent child. "Answer grabbers" don't have it; thinkers do. Once a youngster has cultivated a string of fear-inspired strategies, they become habitual and will interfere with the development of intelligent problem solving. "The scared fighter may be the best fighter, but the scared learner is always a poor learner," according to Holt, who calls this one factor that distinguishes schooling from warfare (1982, p. 93).

One of the few charming and cheerful passages in this rather bleak book is Holt's description of his seventeen-month-old niece playing with his pen, which the determined diarist has with him even at cribside. Her persistent efforts to cap the pen and later to interact with her environment in assorted ways meet often with failure—which daunts her not at all. "Unlike her elders, she is not concerned with protecting herself against everything that is not easy and familiar; she reaches out to experience, she embraces life" (1982, p. 112).

In the section of *How Children Fail* entitled "Real Learning," Holt stresses the need for what I call intellectual empathy; the teacher must try to understand how language about symbols such as numbers and words will be interpreted within the mind of the student. An empathetic teacher will be able to proffer explantions that clarify rather than confuse and that do not overgeneralize (1982, p. 148). Holt also deplores the answer-centered rather than problem-centered focus of many children and teachers alike in what he calls the "Answerland" of school. The rush to cover material is also antithetical to real learning, and Holt recalls at least one experience of success at weaning his students away from defensive strategies and getting them to apply "imagination, resourcefulness, and common sense" to some algebra problems. Unfortunately, he was directed to "speed up the pace," and when he did so, the children resumed their former defensive and nonproductive approaches (1982, p. 156).

In this section Holt raises the question of how we determine when and what students do not understand. He expresses his despair at the discovery that mixed-problem tests indicated that "hardly any of our pupils [understood] anything of what we have been trying to teach them during the year" (1982, p. 177). He distinguishes between real and apparent learning. Real learning, or understanding of something, is indicated for him when, "I can (1) state it in my own words; (2) give examples of it; (3) recognize it in various guises and circumstances; (4) see connections between it and other facts or ideas; (5) make use of it in various ways; (6) foresee some of its consequences; (7) state its opposite or converse" (1982, p. 177). This view of learning puts Holt at odds with those teachers who "have felt all along that their job is to drop, or push, one at a time, little bits of information into those largely empty minds that are moving slowly before them down the academic assembly line" (1982, p. 178).

Likewise, Holt sees knowledge, learning, and understanding as nonlinear phenomena (1982, p. 180). He laments the tendency of educators to view subject areas as linear, a tendency he attributes to the fact that words come "out in single file one at a time." This fact limits our ability to talk or write to a linear model of "word strings," which need to be internalized in our minds into a "working mental model of the universe" that is, by definition, three dimensional. This is real learning.

In another section, entitled "How Schools Fail," Holt questions our motives in education. Do we run schools and classrooms as we do because doing so helps learners and we can see that, or for administrative economy and convenience, or because everyone else runs them this way? In this section he attacks the "testing-examination-marks business" as a "gigantic racket" fraught with dishonesty on the part of the testers and confusion on the part of the tested (1982, p. 240). Teachers want to make it look as if their students know more than they do in order to reflect favorably on their schools and their own performance, as well as to dupe students into thinking that they have learned something. Students want to get the right answer in order to please their teachers, their parents, and even themselves. It was John Holt who made me realize that the College Board Examinations were not, in fact, a natural phenomenon like the changing seasons or the tides, but rather a contrivance of humans for human purposes; in other words, a business. That my tests were also, by definition, flawed was likewise a revelation.

Holt's harshest indictment of the educational conspiracy of administrators, teachers, and parents is his statement that school is "to a very great degree, . . . a place where children learn to be stupid. Curiosity, questions, speculation—these are for outside school, not inside" (1982, p. 263). In the summary in which Holt breaks away from his diaries, he reiterates many of his earlier points and adds some thoughts about the folly of those progressives who believe that there are "good ways and bad ways to coerce children" (1982, p. 295). Holt concludes that all coercion is inevitably partnered by fear and, as Puff, the Dragon Lady who alternately roared and frolicked, I found it valuable to confront this idea.

One student who benefited directly from my reading of Holt was Arthur Klein. Arthur was a very bright and articulate young man whom I taught in College English III. He wrote witty and insightful essays, but they were often on topics of his own choosing rather than mine. There was a hilarious series of compositions about a Jewish chicken and a very erudite and erotic description of Hester Prynne and Arthur Dimmesdale alone together, which were not exactly what I had assigned but were brilliant nonetheless. Arthur's papers were always sloppy, poorly spelled, and late. He himself was in the throes of an awkward adolescence which was immeasurably complicated by the fact that his father, Sol Klein, was Smithfield's art teacher. Sol and I conferred frequently about Arthur since Sol was both worried about him and ambitious for his future. Arthur was not only a talented writer, he was also a promising painter. Of course, Arthur was obligated to rebel against his family's aspirations, and after reading Holt, I decided that Arthur would benefit from a less coercive school than the traditional colleges the Kleins were considering. Therefore, I talked Sol into letting him apply to Goddard College which, at that time, was about as uncoercive as an institution of higher learning could be. Reports from both father and son indicated that Arthur did indeed flourish at Goddard, and I began to inform students and parents of alternative colleges on a regular basis.

A less fortuitous result of my reading Holt at Smithfield was that I became infused with guilt over my role as coercer and tester, a participant in a conspiracy with parents and administrators to manipulate and frighten students literally out of their wits. However, since guilt is a precursor to conscience, my guilt became another ally in my ongoing effort to resist complacency.

HOW CHILDREN FAIL REVISITED

Rereading *How Children Fail*, I no longer find Holt's journal keeping the compulsive activity of an obsessive personality, but rather the record of a careful ethnographer. I wish I had kept a similar record of at least some of the observations I made in A301 and subsequent classrooms I have inhabited. I regret never having kept a teaching journal, not only because such a document would have enormously facilitated the composition of this one, but also because it would have been rewarding and instructive to review the events of those years as recorded by Puff. I feel the regret of any traveler who has visited a fascinating and faraway place, only to return with no photographs or even postcards.

Since I had long ago given my original copy of *How Children Fail* to a colleague, I recently purchased the 1982 reprint of the 1964 edition. This edition is augmented by the author's revisions, which appear as inserts set apart from the original text. In the insert that accompanies the summary, Holt shares his perception of the young educa-

tion students to whom he has often been invited to lecture
subsequent to the success of the first edition of *How
Children Fail*. He recognizes them as extremely fearful
products of an educational system that has replaced their
curiosity, intelligence, and passion with anxiety and a need
for quick and correct answers. In retrospect, he says:

> For heaven's sake, stay out of the classroom until you have got
> over some of your fear of the world. Do something else first.
> Travel, live in different places, do different kinds of work, have
> some interesting experiences, get to know and like yourselves a
> little better, *Get that scared expression off your faces!* Or your
> teaching will be a disaster. (1982, p. 279)

Holt goes on to explain how, like Braithwaite, he himself
didn't start teaching until he was thirty, by which time he
had acquired

> three years of experience as a submarine officer, some in
> combat; I had worked six years in responsible positions in the
> world government movement in the course of which I had given
> about six hundred public lectures; I had lived alone and made
> myself at home, on very little money, in a number of European
> cities; I had ridden a bicycle most of the way from Paris to
> Rome; and in the course of my work for world government, I
> had become something like an extra uncle in about fifty families
> with young children. (1982, p. 280)

Holt acknowledges that had he tried to teach right after
college, *his* teaching would have been a disaster. In retrospect, I am angry that Holt did not share this skeletal
autobiographical data with readers of the original edition.
I am willing to grant that he himself might not have been
aware as a younger man how crucial these preservice years
of life experience were to his developing identity and
performance in the classroom until he began to work with
the education students he deplores. However, it is clear
to me now that a book on teaching written by a teacher

is incomplete without some reconstruction of the individual's preservice life experience to give perspective to the author's classroom work.

Holt's own perspective is decidedly elitist; the author is a product of Exeter and Yale, with extensive experience teaching experimental mathematics in private elementary schools, where he also taught beginning reading. Additionally, he taught English, French, and mathematics to high school students and coached soccer and other sports (Holt, 1967). In short, he is an educated, white, Anglo-Saxon, Protestant male, distanced from the typical working teacher by gender, class, and proximity to the edges of the economic and social abyss that looms ever present in the psyches of many poor, female, and ethnic Americans. This distance is apparent in and between the lines in which he describes as "poor frightened young people" the education students he often addresses, adding that they "need a job and a paycheck right now. School teaching is what they have spent their time and money learning how to do. Other than unskilled labor, what else could they do? How would they find the interesting, demanding, and rewarding work that I had had the good luck to find?" (1982, p. 280) A rereading of Holt informed by considerations of gender and class does not diminish the utility and relevance of much of what he has to say; rather, such a rereading contextualizes the author and the reader and, by so doing, enriches the reading experience.

At the risk of diminishing his own not inconsiderable share of patriarchal power, Holt recognizes that those aspects of schooling that Grumet refers to as the mastery of the "language, the rules, the games, and the names of the fathers" are antithetical to learning (1982, p. 21). Holt's detailed deconstructions of children trying, or not trying, to solve problems, in conjunction with the fact that most of the problems are in math, make parts of this book a rather demanding read for me even today. It is, however, a tribute to the importance and continuing relevance of

Holt's ideas that I am repeatedly struck by the power of the inferences he draws from the behavior he describes. The "Tell-'em-and-test-'em" style of teaching has gained increasing credibility within the educational establishment, which now requires students to pass standardized tests in order to move through elementary school and high school (1982, p. 256). The desire to standardize curriculum, which Holt decries as incompatible with a nonlinear conception of learning and knowledge, is gaining steam.

And Holt's insistence on observing behavior and reflecting on it at leisure in an effort to uncover its meaning is a valuable model for those of us teaching in the 1990s. Equally valuable is Holt's willingness to make explicit in print and in the classroom—and so, available for discussion—the tension and anxiety experienced by learners and teachers alike. And, certainly, acknowledging the paradoxical nature of control is no less useful today, when the gun has replaced the spitball as the weapon of choice in many classrooms, than it was when I taught at Smithfield.

After thirty years of teaching, and living through the untimely illness and death of my husband, the prolonged illnesses and deaths of my parents, and all the attendant disasters that go along with raising children, and then teenagers, in urban America during the 1970s and 1980s, there is only one thing about which I have repeated nightmares: it is losing control of a class at Smithfield High School. I am standing on a chair, shrieking curses and gesticulating frantically at about thirty large teenagers who are milling about room A301, talking, laughing, chewing huge wads of bubble gum, and dribbling basketballs. Two or three exit through the door just as Miss Nolan enters, a grimace of horror widening her eyes and narrowing her lips. When I awaken, sheets sweaty and head throbbing, I am always enormously relieved to return to consciousness and the present, despite whatever catastrophes are currently darkening my life. John Holt's matter-of-fact discussion of the dynamics of control, coercion, and fear remains important.

One of the reasons why Holt is so sensitive to the matter of control is because the classrooms that he describes in *How Children Fail* are teacher-centered rather than collaborative and student-centered. My classroom in A301 was also predominantly teacher-centered; as I explained in chapter 1, in teacher-centered classrooms, the teacher does most of the work and a modicum of silence is desirable. Such a classroom fails to exploit the learners' natural sociability, as well as the social nature of learning. It also fails to utilize the ability of the students to teach one another, which would eliminate some of the opportunities for adult approval or disapproval, which influence behavior so negatively. This is a surprising omission on Holt's part, since one of the book's strengths is the collaborative relationship the author enjoys with his colleague Bill Hull, whose classes Holt observed. In the prefatory acknowledgments, Holt expresses his appreciation to Hull who, "more than anyone, made me look at, see, and think about what was really going on in the classroom and in the minds of the children I was trying to 'teach.'"

Another way in which Holt's book is useful is that in it he describes the behavior in private schools of privileged youngsters of the dominant culture. To many parents, including those who think they can shelter their children from the evils of our educational system by ensconcing them in costly, and hence exclusive, independent schools, *How Children Fail* has much to reveal. Likewise, it should be required reading for those legislators who see in voucher plans, which would make some private schools accessible to poor youngsters, an educational panacea. The students Holt describes who are failing to learn do not suffer from malnutrition, neglect, or the other forms of abuse common to less fortunate youngsters. They are in small classes taught by kindly teachers, and yet, they fail to learn. One is easily able to imagine the plight of less fortunate students in many of our nation's public schools, students who arrive hungry, bruised, and cold and may speak little English. Frightening though it may be, school is, no doubt, a relatively safe haven for many of these youngsters, but neither type of school, private or public, provides most students with a genuine learning experience.

Although in *How Children Fail* Holt fails to offer much insight into how to change the dynamics he deplores, he does serve as a kind of conscience or watchdog, an educational moralist, and a classroom researcher par excellence. For me he was a lookout, the song's "Jackie Paper" to my Puff, pointing out the pirate ships that threatened our boat as we sailed across the sea. However, unlike the faithless Jackie Paper, Holt has remained an enduring companion, who is useful to the mature teacher and parent as well as the neophyte.

6

36 Children: Herbert Kohl

A RETROSPECTIVE RESPONSE

During my fifth year at Smithfield, I felt like Dorothy stranded in Oz and ignorant of how to escape. However, unlike the good witch Glinda, who facilitated Dorothy's flight, Mr. Schwartzman did not respond affirmatively to my repeated requests for a transfer to the newly opened Thomas E. Hill High School in downtown New Haven.

Designed by Eero Saarinen, this architectural showplace was organized around the house plan, with four separate and distinct sections, or houses, each administered by a Head; a bright and talented principal hired via a national search coordinated the entire school. Hill's glamorous new building, intriguing organization, and promise of pedagogical innovation were attractive to many students; however, some objected to the redistricting that uprooted them from their comfortable residential enclaves and set them down in the gritty urban setting where Hill was located, between the railroad tracks, the highway, and a housing project.

Jerry, my friend and neighbor from A303, had begun his administrative career by becoming Assistant Head of East

House. Rhonda Gold, my friend and mentor at Smithfield, headed North House; she was the first and only woman at that level of secondary school administration in New Haven. The heads had been carefully selected and included an Italian-American male, an African-American male, a Jewish-American woman, and a white, Anglo-Saxon, Protestant male. The Head of Hill High's English Department was Sam Downs, a former colleague at Smithfield. A cultured and avuncular fellow, Sam was witty and relaxed. Although he and I disagreed on the educability of many of our students, we had covered the ground often enough to know where each of us stood. I wanted very badly to join the diverse and enthusiastic staff at Hill, so I continued to inundate Mr. Schwartzman with requests for transfer.

Out of the Frying Pan

There were two factors which, I believe, finally moved Mr. Schwartzman to decide that he could, in fact, spare me. First, my fifth year at Smithfield followed my grant-funded summer studies at Wesleyan University, where I had taken a course entitled "The Ethnic Writer in Urban America" taught by the late Dr. George Kent. Kent was an African-American scholar and professor, the first I'd ever known. His broad perspective on literature, as well as his critical acumen and gentle humor, had made the class revelatory and pleasurable. The reading list included several African-American writers of whom I had never heard (W. E. B. DuBois, Ann Petry, Langston Hughes, and Ralph Ellison) and others whose names I knew (Richard Wright and James Baldwin). We also read William Faulkner and Bernard Malamud since, to my amazement, Kent considered them ethnic writers as well. I recall discovering the many layers of literary and historical meaning and linguistic richness in the works we read.

It was like being remembered generously in the will of a relative I hadn't known existed. This class was paired with one called "Psychology and Sociology in Literature of the American Negro," a developmental psychology course overlaid with a consideration of the impact of poverty, segregation, and discrimination on family life.

My best friends in the program were two renegade nuns with whom I debated over lunch cunning strategies for integrating our newfound literary treasures and psychological insights into the curricula at our respective schools. Predictably, in the fall, neither Miss Nolan nor Mr. Schwartzman were receptive to my suggestion that we add selected works by African-American authors to the book closet at Smithfield, but I persisted.

Then, a few weeks before Easter vacation, Ron Gibson's mother protested to Mr. Schwartzman that Twain's use of the word "nigger" in *Huckleberry Finn*, which Ron's General English III class was reading with me, was racist, and that therefore, I must be racist. She was militant, perplexed, and determined that I jettison the book midstream, as it were. Mr. Schwartzman, who I doubt had ever read *Huckleberry Finn*, was extremely upset by her assertive stance. He was not accustomed to mothers of African-American students taking issue with the curriculum; Mrs. Gibson's concern and her active participation in her son's schooling were indications of growing community involvement in education that characterized the late 1960s in New Haven.

It took Ron and me over two tense periods to convince her that *Huckleberry Finn*, and our discussion of it, were part of the fight against racism rather than expressions of it. That this was a simplistic response, I know now, but it was entirely consistent with my reading of *Huckleberry Finn* at that time. My response to that book, like the response that Wayne Booth (1988) details in *The Company We Keep: An Ethics of Fiction*, has been complicated and enriched by the inevitable expansion of my critical conscience and consciousness over the decades. Clearly, however, I was becoming a liability, and soon after the *Huckleberry Finn* incident, Mr. Schwartzman approved my request to transfer to Hill the following fall.

The Honeymoon

At Hill I was assigned to North House, room N102, to work with Rhonda. My journey had finally taken me to a place where I fit in—where the culture was defined by freedom, creativity, and inclusion rather than by repression, rote, and exclusion. There I was asked to supervise student teachers and to select books that actually were bought and taught, and I was liberated forever from my role as enforcer of the dress code. Furthermore, I had just turned twenty-seven and considered myself a mature and defined personality. Being an urban English teacher was now an important part of my identity. The late 1960s was an exciting time to be alive and teaching, and it was the perfect time to read *36 Children*.

In this book, Kohl validates many of the beliefs that I had come to hold while at Smithfield; most notable among these was the firm conviction that it was my responsibility as an English teacher to fight the racism that I now saw as intrinsic to America. Just as I had once believed that literacy was the key to personal fulfillment and that it was my charge to help people enhance their literacy, I now believed that understanding one's own position with respect to race and assuming responsibility for it were the keys to social salvation in America, and it was my job to help people enhance their self-awareness and social consciences—through literature, of course.

In the first and longest section of *36 Children*, called simply "Teaching," Kohl intersperses his recollections of his work with the sixth grade class in Harlem that is the subject of the book with samples of student writing. How

I enjoyed reading of his first days in their classroom, his fears, his decision to lock away the children's record cards unread, his prayer, "Everything must go well; we must like each other" (1967/1988, p. 13). How I relished his gradual winning of the children's confidence, affection, and respect. How confirming I found his rejection of the "flat and uninteresting" readers filled with depictions of pleasant lives and geared to middle class children (1988, p. 19).

Several years earlier, when I had read of Sylvia Ashton-Warner's similar response to her school's readers, I had marveled at her ability to create her own substitutes. Now, reading Kohl, I myself had replaced *Silas Marner* with *The Cool World* and *The Old Man and the Sea* with *Manchild in the Promised Land*. My students were also reading *Native Son*, *The Invisible Man*, and *Black Boy* in addition to the canonical works we had always read. Class discussions had become dynamic, lively, angry forums. For African-American and white students alike, especially the boys, reading had become a means of exploration of the world as they were experiencing it. As Keith Gilyard writes in a passage praising Kohl's work in his own linguistic autobiography, *Voices of the Self: A Study of Language Competence*, "Even though there is little one teacher can do substantially to change many lives, there is . . . great value in encouraging the discussion of community experience within academic environs" (1991, p. 116). Even student essays were becoming personal; it was that year that I read sophomore May Lewis's graphic and dramatic account of how she had delivered her baby alone under the covers, without waking her parents, who were asleep in the adjacent bedroom.

I felt a collegial kinship with Kohl and what Gilyard calls his "workshop in humanistic education" (1991, p. 115). Kohl explores words and myth with his students, validating in the process their own language, and I explored literature and reality with mine, validating their own experience and expressiveness (1988, p. 35). Kohl sees

the evolution of a unit on the History of Man that he
prepares and works on with his class as providing a kind of
spiritual salvation for the children, a way for them to
understand their origins and so, "gain the strength to
persist" (1988, p. 52). I felt similarly as I introduced my
students, Euro- and African-American alike, to the heroes
and villains who people all of American literature.

Kohl takes Holt's criticism of the testing rituals one step
further, for he explains to the children the uses of the
standardized tests, how to follow directions, and how to
attack the different types of questions typical of these
tests. Against the wishes of his principal, he locates and
gives them sample tests. In short, he prepares them for
the reading tests just as middle class students are prepared,
and they do extremely well.

I savored his deconstruction of this powerful mechanism
for the perpetuation of institutionalized racism with his
students, and I gloated over their triumph. The pleasure
I took in this section of *36 Children* was no doubt intensi-
fied by the sudden revelation that for years Mr. Schwartzman had been ordering his secretary to raise grades on the
transcripts of those Smithfield students who attended his
expensive, family-run, private tutoring school which offered
help in Latin, English, foreign languages, science, and
math. No wonder so many of Smithfield's college preparatory students had been getting into such good colleges for
so long. His crime made national headlines and ultimately
cost him the principalship. As "punishment," he was put in
charge of school buses at an annual salary of $30,000,
more than triple mine.

I admired Kohl's efforts to share his world and his life
with his students by inviting them to his apartment on
Friday afternoons, taking them to Harvard to visit the
scene of his undergraduate education, and introducing
them to Judy, his fiancée. On the weekend trip to Harvard, the children surprise Kohl and Judy by preferring to
remain in the safe, clean, and well-equipped motel room,

cozily enjoying an evening of television and games, rather than to do extensive sightseeing (1988, p. 60). As a result of this trip, Kohl gains a deeper appreciation of the grim reality of their daily lives.

I had seen the popular musical *Hair* and I knew my students would enjoy it, so I convinced a colleague to accompany me and two busloads of excited teenagers to a matinée. Upon arriving in New York, we distributed the tickets and told the students that they had an hour for lunch before the performance began. We invited anyone without sightseeing plans to join us at a Greek restaurant on Eighth Avenue and 47th Street. About eight of the shyer students, intimidated by their first visit to New York, took us up on our offer and we shared a pleasant lunch hour. The play was a hit. On the way home, however, after no fewer than six students on my bus threw up all over me and each other, I realized the sort of sightseeing many of them had been doing during lunch hour. It was only then that I remembered the disparity that existed at that time between the drinking age in New York (eighteen) and that in Connecticut (twenty-one). Like Kohl, I had anticipated a zeal for tourism that was eclipsed by the students' other desires and opportunities. They had entered "The Age of Aquarius."

Kohl's insistence on trying to blend his personal and professional life so as to inform the children of the world outside Harlem as well as of the thoughts and feelings inside him—to bridge the supposedly unbridgeable chasm created by differences in race, class, culture, age, and geography—is responsible for one of this book's most moving episodes. The children organize a surprise wedding party for him and "Miss Judy" on the morning of their marriage (1988, p. 164). Like E. R. Braithwaite, Kohl is a kind of living curriculum for his students, inviting them to study him and so, learning from them. During this process of mutual scrutiny, Kohl realizes "how narrow [is] the view from the teacher's desk" (1988, p. 107).

Unlike John Holt, Kohl scatters contextualizing autobiographical data throughout his book, telling the reader
of his own secure Bronx childhood, his happy Harvard
undergraduate experience, and his decision to abandon
graduate studies in philosophy because a life of scholarship was too lonely. He even tells how he meets his future
wife. It was also interesting to read of Kohl's punitive
transfer to Harlem after he confronted the administration
of the first New York City public school in which he taught
with the inadequacy of the school's reading program (1988,
p. vi). Afraid of being forced to leave his new students
whom he is learning to care about, he says, "So I learned
to keep quiet, keep the door of my classroom shut, and
make believe that the class and I functioned in a vacuum,
that the school around us didn't exist" (1988, p. 42). I
recognized my own coping mechanism at Smithfield and
again felt a sense of kinship with Kohl. His personal
revelations were humanizing; Kohl seemed real.

In fact, one of the things I valued most about *36
Children* was that Kohl, like Ashton-Warner, was willing
to acknowledge his errors and faults. For although I was
happier and more confident in my professional life at
Hill than I had been at Smithfield, I realized that many of
my students were not becoming more literate or more
socially responsible as a result of my teaching. Kohl
acknowledges that one boy was "too much for me to
control" (1988, p. 179), a "tough" boy who "shook [Kohl's]
confidence." Like Holt, he admits the classes' inability to
"cover" everything, a concession I found comforting too,
since the more complex our discussions in room N102
became, and the more books I felt we simply had to read,
the less time we had. Near the beginning of his adventure
with the thirty-six children, Kohl explains how the frequent
need for teachers to respond intuitively means "that the
teacher must make mistakes." He adds:

I've said many unkind things in my classroom, hit children in anger, and insulted them maliciously when they threatened me too much. On the other hand, I've also said some deeply affecting things, moved children to tears by unexpected kindnesses, and made them happy with praise that flowed unashamedly. . . . The teacher has to live with his own mistakes as his pupils have to suffer them. Therefore, the teacher must learn to perceive them as mistakes and find direct or indirect ways to acknowledge his awareness of them and his fallibility to his pupils.

The ideal of the teacher as a flawless moral exemplar is a devilish trap for the teacher as well as a burden for the child. (1988, p. 24)

Reading Kohl's confession as well of his manipulation of the constraints governing the acquisition of supplies like books and science and art equipment, helped me to put to rest finally my sense of myself as somehow having to be perfect. I learned how to say, "Gee, I made a mistake. I'm sorry," and, "I don't know; let's look it up somewhere or ask somebody." After five years of teaching, and in a new and less repressive setting, I had reached the point that Kohl reaches after only two years in the classroom. It was better late than never.

The Fire This Time

There is another reason why *36 Children* was appropriate reading while I was at Hill. Like *How Children Fail*, *36 Children* is finally a sad, even tragic, book. True, the first part details Kohl's success in helping the children to express themselves, respect themselves, and expand their world, to learn and flourish after years of intellectual stagnation in schools where adults expected little and gave less. But in the second section of the book called "A Dream Deferred," Kohl describes what happens to the children after they leave his class. Many of them flounder, eventually leaving school altogether. A few, who escape the Harlem schools to special schools or programs for the gifted, achieve limited success that is either short lived or at the expense of their cultural identity. As one child tells Kohl, "One good year is not enough" (1988, p. 205).

In this section Kohl includes letters he and Judy receive from some of the children chronicling their adventures in junior high school. The letters are articulate, poignant, and filled with affection and appreciation. Their authors thank the Kohls for mail and for their gifts of art supplies, books, and stamps. As a kind of counterpoint to these documents are the conversations Kohl hears among his colleagues. For now that he is confident in his own teaching, he no longer feels the need to isolate himself from them. What he hears is disturbing, yet it was familiar to me:

After a while the word "animal" came to epitomize for me most teachers' ambiguous relations to ghetto children—the scorn and the fear, the condescension yet the acknowledgement of some imagined power and unpredictability. I recognized some of that in myself, but never reached the sad point of denying my fear and uncertainty by projecting fearsome and unpredictable characteristics on the children and using them in class as some last primitive weapon. It was pitiful yet disgusting, all the talk of "them," "these children," "animals." (1988, p. 187)

My honeymoon at Hill was, in some senses, abbreviated by the fact that chaos broke out very shortly after I arrived. First there was a teachers' strike. I had chosen not to join the union since its spokespeople were unsuccessful in portraying teaching as the noble calling I had come to see it as. I could not imagine myself striking either in spite of the fact that my meager earnings were still barely enough to sustain us. However, after days of anguished debate, when the strike began, several like-minded colleagues and I honored the picket line, at least partly because we were intimidated by the threats of our unionized colleagues. Our liberated students swarmed through the new and nearby Chapel Square Mall with immediate results. The terrified shop owners called the mayor, who called the negotiators, who promptly settled the strike.

But the end of the strike did not bring an end to upheaval at Hill which was, after all, a microcosm for the city—and the nation—in the late 1960s. The African-American students from the housing project adjacent to the school routinely fought with the Italians, who swaggered nervously over from their neighborhood further west. The Jewish teenagers from Westville trembled on the periphery of the action, hoping to escape unnoticed. The weapons of choice, which seem tame by today's standards, were chains wrapped around fists and an occasional knife.

Our dream school had many doors opening to the street, so it was virtually impossible to keep "outsiders" out and students in. (Had Mr. Saarinen ever been in an urban high school or talked to an urban teenager or teacher?) There were no windows in the classrooms, but glass lined the corridors, providing panoramic views of the surrounding slums. After these windows were repeatedly fragmented by rocks, they were replaced by sheets of plywood. When it rained, leaks in the corridor ceilings gushed water into the halls, literally turning them into rivers. The building was closed in the 1980s, remaining vacant and abandoned until it was finally renovated as office space for a local hospital.

Triggering the fire alarm was the usual signal. Whenever this shrill clarion sounded, we were ordered by our principal to evacuate the building. This resulted in bedlam as teachers and students streamed out through the many doors, with some youngsters fighting and throwing chairs, lunch trays, and assorted other school property. Gradually, different teachers developed different responses. Some dutifully shepherded their students outdoors into certain pandemonium and tried vainly to break up the fighting: "Come on Vernon. Let's go back inside and read." Or, "Gino, let's talk about this after school. Fighting never solves anything." Or, "Melvin, why don't you let me hold that knife for you? You're going to hurt somebody." One of my male colleagues used to let his students leave the building and then lock himself in his classroom. Finally, I ignored the principal's orders to evacuate and tried to contain my students in the relative safety of room N102.

On one memorable occasion I put my arm around a frail, bespectacled young woman, attempting to shield her during her escape from the auditorium where flying books and flashing fists had disrupted an assembly honoring the recently assassinated Dr. Martin Luther King, Jr. "Get your hands off me, you honky bitch!" she snapped, recoiling from my touch. Here was a whole new level of hostility; I didn't even know this student. I was a white teacher, a female adult, and hence, a "honky bitch." Once again, my teaching journey had made me a stranger in a strange land, and this new country was at war.

The students at Hill had lived too long in a fragmented and unjust nation, democratic in rhetoric only, and committed to violence at home and abroad. It was inevitable that they mirror the rebellion and violence around them. At the end of his story Kohl says, "The thirty-six children are suffering from the diseases of our society. They are no special cases; . . . if I have the strength I will be there to rejoice and cry with them, and to add my little weight to easing the burden of being alive in the United States today" (1988, p. 224). Within a short time, the bright and talented new principal as well as several other administrators, including cultured and avuncular Sam, resigned, heading for suburban schools or early retirement. White flight had already begun, changing New Haven's school-age population, economy, and politics for the foreseeable future.

I identified with Kohl's romantic concluding lines, as he

dramatically pledges to pit his "little weight" against the forces that threaten to crush his students, for I was still in many ways the same romantic young woman who had identified with Ashton-Warner's passionate cri du coeur in the preface to *Teacher*. However, unlike Kohl, by the end of the 1969 school year I was two months pregnant, and in New Haven in 1969, a pregnant woman was not allowed to teach after her third month since that was all the school system's insurance covered. So after just two years in the trenches of the embattled Hill High, I was forced to continue my teaching journey elsewhere.

36 CHILDREN REVISITED

My current reading of Kohl finds me noticing details that I did not pick up on at all when I read *36 Children* at Hill. In particular I notice Kohl's way of working with student writers. He avoids grammar corrections, encourages the students to share one another's drafts, writes thoughtful comments that are respectful of student work as it is rather than as it might be, and allows writers to work at their own pace on subjects of interest to them (1988, p. 61). Now I recognize the "uncommon sense" (Mayher, 1990) elements of collaborative learning and process writing that mark his strategies, and I wish I had paid attention to them and tried to adapt some of them to my work at Hill with older students.

Perhaps Kohl's work with writers is so effective because he himself is a writer. He is at work on a philosophy book, *The Age of Complexity*, during the year he describes in *36 Children*. Another point that stands out on rereading Kohl is his metamorphosis from a well-meaning and anxious neophyte to a fulfilled and reflective teacher-writer. Indeed, it is by watching his students write that Kohl is able to overcome his own writer's block and actually complete the philosophy book (1988, p. 192).

As a teacher-writer and scholar of philosophy, Kohl had several authorial voices at his disposal when he wrote *36 Children*. However, he explains in the introduction of the 1988 edition that he chose, "a story form rather than writing a scholarly treatise because I was writing for my students, their parents, and other decent people who cared about social and economic justice. I wanted to make a book that could be read by anyone and not a textbook" (1988, p. viii). Kohl adds that he has included his students' work so that their voices might argue powerfully in their own behalf against those who would blame them for the effects of poverty and racism by labeling them emotionally and culturally deprived, learning deficient, or genetically inferior (1988, p. viii).

A year after his work with this class, Kohl takes a leave of absence to rest, travel to Spain, and write so as to rethink at leisure how best to continue his work with young people (1988, p.192). This, also, was a part of *36 Children* on which I did not focus at the time, although, I, too, was tired and discouraged by some of my teaching experiences. The script I followed was still determined by my gender, class, culture, and age, and it read: "Enter baby" in the place where Kohl's read: "Exit to Spain." I see Kohl, Holt, and Braithwaite as feeling much freer to respond to life situations by improvising or rewriting their scripts than Ashton-Warner, Barrett, and Isenberg. I assume that a younger generation of women will be more adept at improvisation and script revision than I have been.

Like other teacher-writers I have discussed, Kohl too discovers his identity as he confronts "the human challenge of the classroom" (1988, p. 192). He says, "I reached into myself and uncovered a constant core which enabled me to live with my mistakes and hypocrisies, my weaknesses and pettiness; to accept as myself all the many contrary and contradictory things I was. I fought to be more human and feel I succeeded" (1988, p. 192). Kohl's "constant core," which I call identity, is reminiscent of the "still centre" of which Ashton-Warner speaks. The search for it—and discovery of that center—are crucial to adult development, especially to the development of those adults who work with people in a nurturing or generative capacity.

Like Holt, Kohl is an avid observer of children. In fact, he is dismissive of his teacher education at Columbia Teachers' College, claiming that during the year he spent there earning his degree, he "heard no mention of how to observe children, nor even a suggestion that it was of value" (1988, p. 23). He comments:

Without learning to observe children and thereby knowing something of the people one is living with five hours a day, the teacher resorts to routine and structure for protection. The class is assigned seats, the time planned down to the minute, subject follows subject—all to the exclusion of human variation and invention. (1988, p. 23)

Like Holt, Kohl advocates observing students in many contexts, including those in which the teacher is not a major factor.

Kohl's keen observations of the ways in which the children use their unstructured time and how they respond to the stories and ideas he introduces enable him, after relatively little teaching experience, to "hear the situation talking back" which, according to Donald Schön (1983), is one sign of a reflective professional at work (pp. 131-32). The situation tells Kohl to engage the children in studies of etymology and mythology which, as a philosopher, he is well equipped to do. The situation also tells him to bring in books, games, records, and other materials to turn their barren classroom into a learning environment. And, equally impressive, the situation tells Kohl when to withdraw and let the children work alone or in pairs and groups exploring projects and materials that have seized their attention. It took me three decades to learn that sometimes the best way to teach is to stop "teaching" and allow students the time and space in which to learn.

Would that I had been able to absorb this valuable insight when I first read about Kohl's work.

But at the point in my teaching journey at which I encountered Kohl for the first time, I had become both angry and frustrated by the inequities in America that I was just discovering myself, and these feelings structured my response to *36 Children*. I was more sensitive to its political import than to its pedagogical nuances. I shared Kohl's wrath, helplessness, and compassion in a world that is so unfair to so many. And, like Kohl, I felt and still feel powerless to do too much about it. At the end of the introduction to the 1988 edition of *36 Children*, Kohl expresses his belief that

every teacher has a responsibility, as a citizen, to act politically in the name of his or her students for the creation of a just world where children can do rewarding work and live happy lives. If that means being criticized by administrators, becoming involuntarily transferred or even fired, one should be proud of being a troublemaker in a troubled world. (p. x)

I think of Derrick Bell, former Professor at Harvard Law School, who resigned in protest over the fact that there are no tenured African-American women on the Harvard Law School faculty, in spite of the fact that some outstanding candidates had come up for tenure review. Herbert Kohl, Derrick Bell, and others like them have something to say to those of us who may not "make as much trouble" as we should.

7

Teaching Narratives: Literature and Lore

READING TO REMEMBER

I have made teaching narratives, such as the ones I have been discussing here, the subject of this book partly to situate them in a literary and scholarly framework and validate them as a type of autobiographical research that should not be easily dismissed by literary critics or educational theorists (who are often teacher-educators) as merely popular or pragmatic writing. Rather, by recognizing their value as both literature and research, I want to situate them within the discourse of the academy.

In the preceding chapters I have shown how useful the research embodied in these texts was to me as a neophyte and how rewarding it is to reread them from a more experienced and professionally literate perspective. But there is more to these texts than classroom research. At the close of the previous chapter, when we read the words of Herbert Kohl enjoining teachers to stand up for the rights of their students and I refer to Derrick Bell, Kohl is writing within the framework of an established literary tradition, as am I. Let me explain.

In preparation for writing this book, I steeped myself in

autobiographical writing by teachers, reading from Edward
Eggleston's *The Hoosier School-Master*, first published in
1871, to James Nehring's *Why Do We Gotta Do This Stuff,
Mr. Nehring? Notes from a Teacher's Day in School*, published in 1989. My list of teacher narrators included
Conroy (1972), Decker (1969), Gordon (1946), Herndon,
(1968, 1971), Holbrook (1964, 1965), Horton (1990),
Marshall (1968), Neill (1962/1968), Paley (1979, 1981),
Stuart (1973/1992), and Van Til (1983). I became increasingly certain that the books I was reading fit into a
familiar configuration or literary category, but which one?
I had a powerful sense of *déjà vu*, or I should say, more
accurately, *déjà lu* (read). That the patterns of narrative
events, the clear authorial voices, the predictable out-
rages, the moving triumphs organized themselves into a
schema in my mind was not surprising; that this schema
seemed so familiar and yet remained subconscious was
disquieting. I hoped that as I narrowed my focus and
began to consider a few texts closely, I would recall their
literary prototype.

   And that is what happened. My recollections of
studying African-American literature in 1966 with Dr.
George Kent, to which I refer in chapter 4 in connection
with *To Sir, with Love*, prompted me to reflect on a course
called "African American Literature: African American
Autobiography." Professor Arnold Rampersad, an eminent
scholar, teacher, and biographer (Langston Hughes,
Richard Wright, and Arthur Ashe), teaches this course at
Princeton University where, as a recipient of a Mid-Career
Fellowship for selected New Jersey community college
faculty, I audited it in spring 1992. Here I reread some
of the same texts to which Dr. Kent had introduced me
years ago. As I thought anew about these works, I finally
made the connection that I had sensed existed and had
been straining unsuccessfully to make conscious for several
years. In the pages that follow immediately, I will share
with my readers how I corroborated my sense that teaching

narratives do belong to a serious literary tradition, one that purposefully embraces both popularity and pragmatism.

SLAVE NARRATIVES: AUTOBIOGRAPHICAL TESTIMONY

Teaching narratives such as those I discuss here have much in common with slave narratives, the particular form of autobiographical writing that had its genesis in the despicable institution of slavery in this country. Teaching narratives are plainly told by angry authors who describe the suffering of a disempowered constituency in the hope of ending that suffering. They are structured around crises of literacy, identity, and control and operate within constraints and conventions that are politically determined. Let me hasten to clarify that by recognizing the similarities between these narrative types, I do not mean in any way to suggest that the problems faced by teachers and students are the same as those of slaves, human beings who are the legal property of other people, who exist only as chattels to be used and abused in every conceivable way. However, as I shall explain later, it is useful to compare the *narratives* of teachers with those written by ex-slaves. But first, I will briefly discuss the relevant context and characteristics of the slave narrative.

According to Henry Louis Gates, Jr., who edited *The Classic Slave Narratives*, a volume published in 1987 and containing accounts of the lives of Olaudah Equiano (1814), Mary Prince (1831), Frederick Douglas (1845), and Linda Brent (1861):

One of the most curious aspects of the African person's enslavement in the New World is that he and she wrote about the severe conditions of their bondage within what with understatement came to be called "the peculiar institution." In the

long history of human bondage it was only the black slaves in
the United States who—once secure and free in the North, and
with the generous encouragement and assistance of northern
abolitionists—created a *genre* of literature that at once testified
against their captives and bore witness to the urge of every black
slave to be free and literate. Hundreds of ex-slaves felt
compelled to tell their tales on the anti-slavery lecture circuit in
the North and in the written form of the autobiographical
narrative. As several scholars have shown, there is an inextrica-
ble link in the Afro-American tradition between literacy and
freedom. And this linkage originates in the slave narratives.
(p. ix)

Accordingly, as Rampersad explained in the remarks with
which he introduced the slave narratives, their authors are
writing to testify against the institution of slavery, to bear
witness to its evils rather than to focus exclusively on the
self. It is slavery that is at the center of these pieces, and
this distinguishes them from much other autobiographical
composition in which the self is, indeed, at the heart of the
writing.

The ex-slave authors wrote for a specific audience, the
northern abolitionists, often Quaker congregations and
sympathetic others here and in England, who, they hoped,
would further the cause of ending slavery. The authors of
slave narratives not only directed their writing to a particular readership, but saw themselves as representing or
speaking for those blacks yet in bondage, illiterate by
virtue of the same laws that enslaved them.

The circumstances under which the authors of slave
narratives achieved literacy are usually an important part
of their stories since literacy is, as Gates, indicates above,
the crucial link to freedom. In addition, slaves learned to
read and write at considerable personal risk to themselves
and whoever helped them; literacy really was an achievement, requiring courage, intelligence, and perseverance,
which were, not coincidentally, the same characteristics
required for escape. The literate slave was, by definition,

heroic. The exhortations of the male former slave authors recall Patrick Henry's famous words, "Give me liberty or give me death!"

In *Black Women Writing Autobiography: A Tradition within a Tradition*, Joanne M. Braxton sets out to transform "our understanding of the slave narrative" by considering the question, "How did slave women shape their experience into a different kind of literary language?", and in so doing, integrating the lives and scholarship of black women into the critical perspectives defining African-American literature (1989, p. 19). She writes:

> Traditionally, the 1845 *Narrative of the Life of Frederick Douglas, An American Slave, Written by Himself* is viewed as the central text in the narrative genre. Based on this narrative, the critic Robert Stepto has defined the primary Afro-American archetype as that of the articulate hero who discovers the links among freedom, literacy, and struggle. Stepto's definition disregards the narrative experience of the articulate and rationally enlightened female slave, probably because few slave women wrote narratives. Women's experiences are seldom related firsthand, but slave women are often represented in accounts of slave men as mothers and nurturers (generally of their own) or, often as degraded and dehumanized individuals who have lost their self-respect and self-esteem. I propose that such women should be brought forth from this obscurity, that we consider as a counterpart to the articulate hero the archetype of the outraged mother. She is a mother because motherhood was virtually unavoidable under slavery; she is outraged because of the intimacy of her oppression. (1989, p. 19)

Clearly, slave women, who were sexually exploited for pleasure or breeding purposes, wrested from their parents, husbands, and often their children, required to nurture white children often at the expense of caring for their own, and expected to work long and hard to avoid cruel punishment, had cause to be angry.

Braxton describes at least one other way in which the narrative of the outraged mother differs from that of the

articulate hero. The former is, like Harriet Jacobs in
Incidents in the Life of a Slave Girl, likely to "celebrate the
cooperation of all the people, slave and free, who make
her freedom possible" (Braxton, 1989, pp. 19-20). The
latter is more likely to portray himself as a solitary, heroic
figure, conforming to the notions of male heroism preva-
lent at the time. Braxton explains the origins of these
contrasting perspectives in the circumstances governing the
life in captivity of male and female slaves. To do this
she cites Valerie Smith's introduction to the Schomburg
Library's edition of *Incidents* in which Smith explains
that "women slaves were more likely than men to be tied
to the plantation by the demands of childcare; moreover,
men were more likely than women to be sold separately
from their offspring" (Braxton, 1989, p. 20). Smith feels
that these factors would enable male slaves to conceive of
themselves as self-sustaining and isolated figures in their
escape. Braxton also mentions the presence in some narratives by both women and men of a grandmother figure,
a wise and supportive elder who provides inspiration, a
good example, and practical assistance (1989, p. 38). For
female narrators, this grandmother offers a "bonding
opportunity" as well.

Authors of slave narratives also address issues of
identity, like naming and paternity, which were rendered
exceedingly problematic and doubly significant under
slavery. And like the plantation culture that birthed it, the
slave culture was extremely stratified socially, so issues of
social class resonate throughout the writings of ex-slaves
even if they do not directly address them. And of course,
in order to bear witness, the authors of slave narratives
must describe in detail those incidents of cruelty, abuse,
and suffering that filled their daily lives as slaves. It also
falls to them to point out the un-Christian nature of
slavery and the hypocrisy that allowed such an institution
to flourish in a civilized and God-fearing country such as
the United States.

In spite of her or his valor, brains, and determination, the author of a slave narrative was usually not a famous person but rather unknown and, of course, uneducated. These authors were often impeded in their storytelling by the need to protect the people who had facilitated their escape; the most exciting and dramatic details of how they left captivity, eluded recapture en route north, and finally reached safe havens simply could not be revealed. By this necessity the narratives are sometimes filled with gaps and what may appear to be distortions of the truth. In fact, in order to escape, the slave had to manipulate the truth and the constraints that literally confined her or him, and so had to be something of a trickster, all the while seeming artless and naive.

After the victory of the north in the Civil War, slavery was, in fact, abolished rendering the genre that bore witness to it no longer politically necessary. African-American writers were now free to turn their attention to other forms, and they did. However, voices of the ex-slave authors echo powerfully throughout African-American literature to this day, shaping, defining, layering, and refining it. The legacy of the slave narratives is apparent especially, but not only, in African-American autobiographical writing. Classics like Richard Wright's *Black Boy* (1937), Maya Angelou's *I Know Why the Caged Bird Sings* (1969), and Alex Haley's *The Autobiography of Malcolm X* (1964) are enriched and often electrified by descriptions of dawning literacy, crises of naming, outraged maternity, and heroic isolation before the protagonist finally reinvents her- or himself in freedom.

With this necessarily brief contextualization and characterization of the slave narrative as a guide, I now return my attention to the teaching narratives which are the real subject of my efforts here. I will point out some of the ways in which autobiographical writings by teachers such as those which I am considering in this book are like slave narratives and so constitute a literary genre of their own.

TEACHING NARRATIVES AS TESTIMONY

Like slave-narrators, teacher-narrators are usually politically motivated; teacher authors use their own experience to bear witness to terrible, ludicrous, or simply counterproductive things that happen within schools. Ashton-Warner reports on the uselessness of the prescribed reading texts; Kaufman satirizes the self-defeating bureaucracy and ineptitude of school administrators as well as the inadequate facilities and overwhelming teacher workload; Braithwaite dramatizes the insidiousness of racism and classism in the ranks of teachers and students; Holt blames teachers and tests for student fear and failure; and Kohl condemns teachers, schools, and society as a whole for "crushing" the spirits and minds of African-American youngsters. Their books are filled with descriptions of incidents that were detrimental to students.

Like the ex-slave authors, teacher-writers are representing an inarticulate constituency, children and teenagers, who suffer as a result of the failures of our educational system and the people who prescribe and implement its policies in a society which routinely devalues children. Perhaps because they concern themselves with children who are, after all, "womens' work," and because so many of them are themselves women, teachers have also been devalued by this same society (Grumet, 1988, p. 58). Understandably then the voices of teachers, like those of children, have been muted, even stifled, in the debates about schooling.

Also like the ex-slave authors, teachers themselves are former students, marked for better or for worse by their years on the other side of the desk. And like Brent, Douglas, Prince, and Equiano, the teacher-authors have a specific audience in mind for their narratives; it is, as stated in an earlier citation by Kohl, "students, parents, and other decent people who care about social and economic justice" (1988, p. viii). Of course, educators are among these "decent people." These simply written and dramatic narratives are intended to have broad popular appeal, to move a readership to effect changes in our educational institutions. For this reason they often focus on the authors' classroom experiences rather than on their preprofessional lives or personal development.

All the teacher-authors I can think of, men and women alike, speak as "outraged mothers," for they are eloquent in defense of their students, whom they try to nurture and protect in a hostile environment. As I indicated earlier, they are generative people who have assumed responsibility for fostering the intellectual, emotional, and spiritual development of those in their charge.

Like the male slave authors—but regardless of gender —teacher-authors are frequently heroic. Often isolated among unsympathetic colleagues, they struggle alone against great odds and at considerable risk to teach and to learn themselves. When a mentor like Kaufman's Bea Schacter or Braithwaite's A. Florian does materialize, teacher-authors are quick to bond, as did the slave women who were fortunate enough to have access to a grandmother figure. And, like the female ex-slave writers, in their narratives, teacher-authors are generous with praise for those who have helped them.

Slave narratives centralize the achievement of literacy; teaching narratives often centralize the neophyte's achievement of control and community in the classroom, what researcher Patricia Sikes calls a "critical incident" (1985, p. 33). Teachers also write of the achievement of literacy by their students, including portions of their writing, demonstrating their newly acquired accomplishment. Ashton-Warner's account of the success of her "organic reading" method is especially vivid. Of course, to enable others to achieve or improve literacy in school often requires manipulation of constraints, artfulness, and perserverance on the part of both teacher and learner.

Naming is also an issue in both types of narrative. The

ex-slave must often rename her- or himself when beginning
life as a free person. Teachers write of how their students
address them in different ways, from Braithwaite's insistence on "Sir" to Barrett's adjustment to "Teach," and for
many, naming is an important aspect of the development
and recognition of a professional identity. Likewise, what
teachers call their students is revealing. And the metaphors which identify or name philosophies of education
and pedagogical theories are also embedded in some
teaching narratives. Class biases permeate the writings of
teachers and, like the class biases of the former slave
authors, they are often unacknowledged.

Slave-narrators are, by necessity, evasive. Yet at the
same time they must be credible, moving their readership
to action. Teacher-writers are also evasive, often fictional-
izing their experiences, changing names and dates, omitting
recognizable people and events or drastically altering them
in the telling. Just as the slave narratives were written
after the narrator had escaped from slavery, many teaching
narratives are written by those who have left the profession.

TEACHER-AUTHORS: TESTIFIERS
OR TINKERERS?

While slavery was finally abolished, nothing and no one
has managed to end the miseducation that many children
and adolescents have experienced routinely since education was institutionalized into schooling. In fact, there
are many signs that the plight of people in schools is
worsening rapidly. So, teacher-writers continue to testify,
articulating their occasional successes in the face of great
obstacles and highlighting the struggles of their students in
what continues to be, for many, a hostile environment.
But unlike the slave narratives which have finally achieved
academic legitimacy and been incorporated into the canon

by many academics in several disciplines and which shape and enliven the work of novelists, poets, dramatists, and other writers even today, the teaching narrative is frequently disparaged by university-based educators as the lowly, popular, and worst of all, pragmatic stepchild of theoretical research.

As I have indicated, as a beginning teacher these books sustained me. However, my desperate and, at first, uncritical reliance on these testimonials raises the important question of their nature and validity as examples of what William H. Schubert calls teacher lore (1991, p. 212). Even if teachers' testimony is recognized as a valid form of autobiographical protest literature, how is it viewed and used by teacher educators? Among the educators who describe and evaluate teacher lore are Stephen North (1987), Donald Schön (1983), Rita Brause and John Mayher (1991), Robert Welker (1992), and Marilyn Cochran-Smith and Susan L. Lytle (1990). An examination of their considerations and conclusions follows.

North defines teacher lore as pragmatic and experiential, hence open to anything "that works" and without a mechanism for dropping something that no longer "works." In addition, he complains, contributions to lore must be "framed in practical terms as knowledge about what to do"; if they are not, they will be changed by "tinkering" practitioners who are always trying to make them work better (1987, p. 25). According to North, lore is embodied in rituals like Miss Nolan's and my persistent use of the red pencil, writing such as appears in textbooks, and, above all, talk, which he views as the practitioner "community's lifeblood" (p. 33). The talk to which he refers is the exchange of classroom experiences, a given wherever we congregate, and a hallmark of the written teaching narrative.

It is tempting to dispose of North's argument by referring to the work of linguist Deborah Tannen (1992), who distinguishes between the talk of women and that of men, pointing out how their different ways of talking often lead to misunderstanding. The teacher talk to which North alludes in this essay is very clearly, among other things, "woman talk," which is valuable at least as much for its utility in maintaining community as for the information it imparts (Tannen, 1992, p. 76). That "rapport-talk" rather than "report-talk" should be the dominant mode of discourse among teachers, most of whom are women, is hardly surprising. Conversely North frames his discussion of practitioners in the technically rational language of science (and men). Speaking of problems and solutions, he asks that practice become inquiry so that it can "contribute to lore" by producing "new knowledge" (1987, p. 33). For him, practice becomes inquiry only

a) when the situation cannot be framed in familiar terms, so that any familiar strategies will have to be adapted for use;
b) when, although the situation is perceived as familiar, standard approaches are no longer satisfactory, and so new approaches are created for it;
c) when both situation and approach are non-standard. (1987, p. 33)

In fact, it was because of their departure from the prevailing culture at Smithfield that I found the teacher-authors so appealing. They were quick to change or discard existing stratagems and materials that didn't enhance learning or improve the quality of the student's school experience. Likewise, they tried new approaches that often failed to facilitate learning and so, disappointed, they then abandoned them. It would be grossly inaccurate to describe Ashton-Warner's creation of culturally specific readers and Herbert Kohl's units on mythology and etymology as "tinkering." In fact, several of the teacher-authors I have discussed did perform the intense, systematic, and ethical kind of classroom research advocated by Brause and Mayher (1991, p. 46). Moreover, they reported on it and I found inspiration in their well-told stories.

Schön considers the role of teacher as expert from both a historical and epistemological vantage point (Welker, 1992; Schön, 1983). To begin, he summarizes the tenets of Positivism and its offspring Technical Rationality:

First, there was the conviction that empirical science was not just a form of knowledge but the only source of positive knowledge of the world. Second, there was the intention to cleanse men's minds of mysticism, superstition and other forms of pseudoknowledge. And finally, there was the program of extending scientific knowledge and technical control to human society, to make technology, as Compte said, "no longer exclusively geometrical, mechanical or chemical, but also and primarily political and moral." (1983, p. 32)

Schön cites the growing dissatisfaction with an exclusively technical rational approach that characterized professionalism in the first two-thirds of this century; conventional scientific strategies have failed—miserably and expensively—in such vital areas as city planning, social work, education, and psychology, where unique cases and conflicting paradigms confound the professional's ability to select and apply the appropriate theory and then neatly solve the problem (1983, p. 41).

Instead, Schön reconceptualizes the traditional relationship between professional and client or, for purposes of this discussion, teacher and student. His teacher researches and reflects in the very process of teaching, maintaining an open and inquiring stance and relying on an acquired repertoire of classroom experience "to hear the situation talking back" (1983, pp. 131-32). As such, she becomes an explorer and learner, escorting the student through uncharted territory. To most effectively accompany the teacher on this joint academic adventure, the student, according to Schön, must be willing to see the "limits of expert knowledge" and must also "cultivate competence in reflective conversation with the [teacher,] stimulating [her] to reflect on [her] own knowledge-in-practice" (1983, p. 302).

To "enhance the practitioner's capacity for reflection-in-action," Schön suggests what he calls "reflective research," of which there are four types:

Frame analysis, the study of ways in which practitioners frame problems and roles, can help practitioners to become aware of and criticize their tacit frames. Description and analysis of images, category schemes, cases, precedents, and exemplars can help to build the repertoires which practitioners bring to unique situations. A most important kind of research has to do with the methods of inquiry and the overarching theories of phenomena, from which practitioners may develop on-the-spot variations. And practitioners can benefit from research on the process of reflection-in-action itself. (1983, p. 309)

Welker's notion of the teacher is similar to Schön's; he goes so far as to juxtapose the teacher as expert and the romantic critics, among whom he includes Holt and Kohl (1992, p. 71). In the latters' classrooms and in their writings, the teacher is learner, not expert, actively involved in classroom research and "sensitive to the social and political responsibilities of the school." Welker notes that their "insights into classroom life may have been their most lasting contributions" (1992, pp. 77-78).

It is important to view expertise in a critical, comprehensive, and complex way that is appropriate to the postmodern world in which students and teachers find themselves today. Ours is a world both enriched and complicated by diversity, technology, and an unprecedented amount of information. Accordingly, Welker cites teacher-educator John Goodlad's (1990) recent observation that "education is a special profession, one whose standards of practice are not to be constrained in the conventional appeals to detached reason and professional autonomy" (Welker, 1992, p. 132).

It follows that Welker's expanded view of educator

expertise leads him to consider the implications of the fact that "historically teaching has been the province of women," subject to sexism and, regrettably, prone to counteracting trends in the search for "more masculine and patriarchal senses of craft" (1992, p. 132). A more positive, if belated, result of the preponderance of women in teaching is the recognition of feminist pedagogy, or what Nel Noddings refers to as the "caring relation" or "interpersonal reasoning" (1991, p. 165). The protagonists of the teaching narratives I have considered here, male and female alike, embody the principles of feminist pedagogy in their interactions with their students, even while predating the terminology by decades.

In Marilyn Cochran-Smith and Susan Lytle's article, "Research on Teaching and Teacher Research: The Issues that Divide" (1990), the authors explore and expand the definition of teacher research. According to their abstract:

Neither interpretive nor process-product classroom research has foregrounded the teacher's role in the generation of knowledge about teaching. What is missing from the knowledge base for teaching, therefore, are the voices of the teachers themselves, the questions teachers ask, the ways teachers use writing and intentional talk in their work lives, and the interpretive frames teachers use to understand and improve their own classroom practices. Limiting the official knowledge base for teaching to what academics have chosen to study and write about has contributed to a number of problems, including discontinuity between what is taught in universities and what is taught in classrooms, teachers' ambivalence about the claims of academic research, and a general lack of information about classroom life from a truly emic perspective. (p. 2)

In the course of arguing for the validity of teacher research as opposed to university-based research which they call "research on teaching," the authors say, "Regarding teacher research as a mere imitation of university research is not useful and ultimately condescending. It is more use-

ful to consider teacher research as its own genre, not
entirely different from other types of systematic inquiry
into teaching, yet with some quite distinctive features"
(1990, p. 4). A consideration of some of the characteristics
of the "new genre" reveals it as the home of the teaching
narratives under discussion in this book.

Cochran-Smith and Lytle describe the standards for
methodological rigor that are used to determine the
validity of teacher research. One, of course, involves
research questions. They point out that unlike the research questions in university-based classroom research,
teacher researchers formulate questions arising from their
day-to-day experiences. They add that while these questions may not themselves be "framed in the language of
educational theory, they are indeed about discrepan-
cies between theory and practice" (1990, p. 6). While the
teacher who framed the question may not have done so out
of a desire to generalize from her experience, the resulting
research may indeed be applicable to many other situations. Furthermore, "embedded in the questions of
teacher-researchers are many other implicit questions
about the relationships of concrete particular cases to
more general and abstract theories of learning and teaching" (1990, p. 6). The authors go on to establish the value
of specific context as opposed to generalizeability; the
former is a characteristic, often much maligned, of teacher
research and the latter, a characteristic of university-based
research. We need insight into what is effective in particular classrooms as opposed to laws that attempt to prescribe
for all classrooms. In fact, they cite Holt's mandate that
teachers should question and observe in their own classrooms, which he added to the 1988 edition of *How Children Fail* in support of this point.

In the discussion of theoretical frameworks that is part
of their description of the "emerging genre of teacher
research," the authors note that traditionally a distinction
has been made between "professional knowledge and

educational theory" (1990, p. 7). They posit alternatives to this oppositional juxtaposition by citing Sanders and McCutcheon who claim that "professional knowledge essentially is theoretical knowledge" (Cochran-Smith and Lytle, 1990, p. 7); they recap, albeit not very enthusiastically, North's aforementioned position; and they themselves favor the views of Shulman whose work, "suggests that the base for teaching is complex, encompassing knowledge of content, pedagogy, curriculum, learners and their characteristics, educational contexts, purposes and values and their philosophical and historical grounds" (Cochran-Smith and Lytle, 1990, p. 8).

They feel this view allows for the teacher researcher to be both the user and generator of theory, an authoritative contributor to the knowledge base of teaching. Accordingly, they see the "truly emic view" of the classroom teacher as different from that of an outside observer, even if that observer is a seasoned ethnographer. Clearly, teaching narratives epitomize teacher-based research, the many faceted "emerging genre," heralded by Cochran-Smith and Lytle. Their authors, who have spoken for all of us for well over a century, often as the only teachers whose voices sounded outside the classroom doors, are teacher-researchers par excellence.

Part of Cochran-Smith and Lytle's argument focuses on the enormous value of "self-directed inquiry" about their own teaching for the researcher herself as well as for her students. The teacher becomes a theorist, ethnographer, writer, and resource, and forms part of a network of other similarly blessed individuals. Her acumen as a reader and critic is sharpened, while her students, their intellectual appetites whetted by inquiry and collaboration, are intrinsically motivated to read, write, and talk. Just as the teacher-researcher and her students are transformed by the process of inquiry, so the academic community is enriched as it becomes the recipient of detailed case studies embedded in culturally accurate accounts. Unfortunately, the transformative potential of the research process will only be appreciated by some teachers, and only some academics will value the usefulness of the resulting narratives.

In spite of the obvious advantages of teacher research as envisioned by Cochran-Smith and Lytle, the inability of many teachers to articulate exactly how they have gone about providing students with the opportunity to learn is noted by Welker, North, Brause and Mayher, and Schön. In fact, Brause and Mayher stipulate the "sharing of outcomes in professional contexts" as a quality of "effective and productive teacher-research" (1991, p. 209). The uncharacteristic silence in this area of many in our profession makes the testimony of the teacher-authors who could and did bear witness to their own classroom work, as well as to that of their students, a valuable legacy indeed, and one worthy of continued study.

TEACHER-EDUCATORS: TRUSTEES OF THE LEGACY

Many teacher-educators now recognize the value of teaching narratives; two years ago, the National Council of Teachers of English honored Mike Rose's *Lives on the Boundary: The Struggles and Achievements of America's Underprepared* (1989) with its prestigious Russell Award. In May 1991 the same organization devoted an entire special issue of *English Education* to Jenifer Smith's "Setting the Cat among the Pigeons: A Not So Sentimental Journey to the Heart of Teaching" (1991). When I was in graduate school, I was assigned *"The Having of Wonderful Ideas" and Other Essays on Teaching and Learning* (1987) by Eleanor Duckworth, another teacher-writer-researcher.

In *Emerging as a Teacher* by Robert V. Bullough Jr., J. Gary Knowles, and Nedra Crow, the authors present the case histories of six first year teachers in an attempt to determine the preservice constructs and experiences as well as the personal characteristics that facilitate one's eventual transition from neophyte to fulfilled and productive teacher. The data for the case histories are gathered through interviews, journals, and seminar notes. In arguing for the case study method, the authors cite Noddings and Shulman, both advocates of the "unique pedagogical power of narrative" (1989, p. 12). However, the case studies themselves, although instructive, are dull and easily forgettable. They fail to make the leap from studies to stories. Nonetheless, the authors' point is well taken; it is crucial for preservice teachers to examine their lives, making conscious their assumptions about race, gender, and class, as well as their constructs of teachers and teaching.

As I have detailed, my own preservice persona, the "princess as New Critic," was of limited utility at Smithfield High School. Furthermore, this identity was very much a social and cultural construction, aspects of which have been amply documented here as well as in *Young, White, and Miserable: Growing Up Female in the Fifties* by sociologist Wini Breines (1992). My ignorance of the socially and culturally constructed nature of my identity was compounded by the fact that Smithfield offered no support for the first act of the existential comedy of trial and error that was my desperate struggle to reconstruct myself into a more effective person. Nor was Smithfield any more receptive to the second act of this production, during which I wrestled alone against "commonsense" notions of pedagogy, curriculum, and Smithfield's culture to learn new ways to think about teaching and being a teacher (Mayher, 1990). Teaching narratives offer the aspiring teacher a chance to fantasize about actually being a teacher after thousands and thousands of hours of being a student. How different my experience at Smithfield would have been if some of these personal and professional issues had been addressed during the course of my preservice education. How I would have relished the chance to explore them with peers and mentors, to study my part before I was thrust onto the stage of room A301 to perform on my own before critics and a live audience.

According to teacher-educator E. Wayne Ross:

Reconstruction of experience in teacher education includes attending to ways in which personal biography constitutes both the content and consequence of reflective thinking. Reconstruction of self-as-teacher focuses on helping teachers become more aware of how setting and personal history influence their practice by shaping their beliefs, values, feelings, and felt needs. (1992, p. 187)

Although Ross is arguing here for collaborative action research, his conclusions also speak powerfully for a systematic consideration of teaching narratives in teacher education programs where they can be used to make explicit and therefore discussable key autobiographical and professional constructs.

And in "Facilitating Teacher Personal Theorizing," teacher educator Gail McCutcheon notes:

A teacher's theory of action consists of sets of beliefs, images, and constructs about such matters as what constitutes an educated person, the nature of knowledge, the society and psychology of student learning, motivation, and discipline. Because of differences among teachers, these theories vary from one teacher to the next. One difference is in their personal experience before becoming teachers. Through such experiences people make sense of the world, and the reservoir of these experiences is one source of teachers' theories of practice. Experiences while growing up, going to school, working, and interacting with people and the world shape our knowledge and attitudes. Because these experiences and the meanings individuals make of them differ, teachers' theories of practice differ. Theories of action also differ because of differences in the context of teaching. (1992, p. 191)

As her argument progresses, McCutcheon explains that many of the assumptions underlying teachers' theories are tacit, "not consciously held, reflected, or deliberated upon" (1992, p. 196). She continues to advocate "bringing these theories to a conscious level" as an important goal of teacher education. The utility of the narratives of teachers as individual and collective consciousness raisers is, of course, well understood by William H. Schubert, leader of the Teacher Lore Project at the University of Chicago, who sees them as a "genuine and neglected form of inquiry. Through interaction with their stories our own stories [a]re more fully revealed to us" (1991, p. 223).

As I explained earlier, a part of my own story that was illuminated by my reading of several teaching narratives was my own sexuality in professional contexts. Unlike the authors of most other literature germane to teaching and learning, many of the teacher-authors, like Kaufman and Braithwaite, who write of experiences in secondary schools, *do* broach this subject. They make explicit the fact that teachers need to behave as nurturing women and men regardless of the caprices of Eros, the vicissitudes of their personal lives, or the tight jeans of the student in the third row. And once the subject of teacher sexuality is introduced, the teacher educator can help prospective and developing teachers to make it a topic for discussion with partners, in groups, in journals, essays, and at conferences, a topic for further reflection at rest or in action. Forewarned is, after all, forearmed.

Even a hasty perusal of the daily newspaper reveals that sexual harassment and abuse of students by teachers occur in every possible permutation in the ivied halls of the nation's most prestigious preparatory schools as well as in the doll corners of subsidized inner city day care centers. Postsecondary and postgraduate institutions are, likewise, not immune to the impact of the liaisons dangereuses between sex and power that can play havoc with teaching and learning. And teachers themselves, especially young ones, are vulnerable to the occasional manipulation and/or admiration of students. In the teaching narratives, as in the slave narratives, one's sexuality is problematic unless, like Harriet Jacobs or E. R. Braithwaite, one contrives to manage it as well as possible under the circumstances. But at least in these narratives teacher sexuality is acknowledged, opening the door a crack to let in the scents and sounds of the real world.

To encourage further exploitation by teacher-educators of the rich lode of teaching narratives, I am going to suggest some additional ways in which the narratives can supplement theoretical, historical, psychological, and philosophical reading in education curricula. My experience as a graduate student revealed that, for a variety of reasons, not all students of education are enthusiastic or facile readers. While this in no way disqualifies them from teaching, it does pose certain problems for them as students as well as for the teacher-educator who wishes to share the profession's literature with them. The straightforwardness of the teaching narratives combined with their vivid description and engaging plots make them accessible to the hurried, the reluctant, the plodding, or the second language reader. I do not mean to imply that only these readers should study the teaching narratives, or that these readers should read only the narratives.

Another problem reader is often someone who is, like me, a Jungian extrovert and needs the presence of others to confirm her or his sense of existence. How is it that as an extrovert, I have always spent long, happy, comfortable hours alone with a book? According to Dorothy Rowe, the British psychologist who introduced me to Jung, an isolated extrovert can survive by relating to the characters in books (1988, p. 54). Hence, the extroverted reader will seek out narratives that have characters and may go so far as to avoid the less sparsely populated genres. In keeping with this, Rowe says:

Introverts, as they meditate upon, or digest their observations and experience, are developing some theory to explain what they have observed and experienced. They find great satisfaction out of developing a total explanation, and can feel satisfied if they can understand and explain a problem, even if there is nothing in their explanation which allows them to solve it. Extroverts get very impatient with introverts over this. Extroverts like to get on and do things. They prefer action to explanation. (1988, pp. 120-21)

Like all students, the students of teacher-educators come in both varieties. Ideally, people integrate their personalities to the point that they are neither dependent groupies nor obsessive theoreticians. However, I am convinced that part of the attraction of the teaching narratives for me initially stemmed from my isolation and loneliness at Smithfield.

Wayne Booth speaks to me when, in *The Company We Keep: An Ethics of Fiction*, he writes:

I think of myself not as an atomic unit bumping other atoms but as a *character*—as someone doing my best to enact the various roles "assigned" me—boundaries between the others who are somehow both outside and inside me and the "me" that the others are "in". As Gregory Bateson puts it in that fine, strange, rambling book *Steps to an Ecology of Mind* (1972), I am not bounded by my skin. Rather, as a character I am a kind of focal point in a field of forces . . . or as we used to say, a creature made in the image of God and hence essentially *affiliated*, joined to others and more like them than different from them. To be *joined*, in other words, is my primary, natural condition. (1988, pp. 239-40)

Not surprisingly, as Booth goes on to describe ethical criticism, he uses the metaphor of friendship between reader and author to define their relationship; the authors we choose to read are, in fact, "the company we keep." While his discussion focuses primarily on fictional works, his analogy is useful in defining the relationship that teacher-readers ought to have with teacher-authors. It is often the obligation of teacher-educators to make the introductions.

For the preservice teacher who has little, if any, classroom teaching experience, the teaching narratives are an invaluable resource, providing lively and authentic glimpses of a variety of school cultures, administrative modes, physical plants, work loads, and professional stances. In all of them, theories of teaching and learning are embedded in the pedagogy of the protagonists; however, in some testimonies, like those of Kaufman and Braithwaite, the pedagogy is "commonsense," reflecting the narrators' conception of teaching as transmission (Mayher, 1990). It is useful for students of education to learn to recognize poorly premised pedagogy, especially as practiced by hardworking and well-meaning teachers. In fact, the deconstruction of some of the teaching narratives on pedagogical-theoretical grounds is one of their chief values for inexperienced people who need to contextualize their new theoretical knowledge but lack the practice to enable them to do so easily.

That teaching narratives are often exemplars of "how not to" rather than "how to" does *not* make them less valuable, but rather dictates the way we read them. Just as Robert Coles reads the doctoring stories of William Carlos Williams with his medical students at Harvard, so can teacher-educators use teaching narratives to facilitate the initiation of neophytes into the profession (1989, p. xvii). I am certain that if contemporary medical students can distinguish the enduring verities of doctoring from any outdated treatments Williams describes, students of education can learn to critique their professional literature, recognizing and cradling the baby while pouring out the bath water.

Williams had an advantage as a doctor-author in that he was really a poet who practiced medicine; similarly, teacher-educators can use the teaching narratives to help education students find their voices as poets, chroniclers, researchers, story tellers, critics, and biographers. According to Grumet, this is no easy task in the patriarchal hierarchy of schooling where teachers are "deprived of the opportunity to design the structure of their own lives, their own work", and instead committed to acting out "the maternal ethos of altruism, self-abnegation, and repetitive labor [which] has denied the power of narrative to teachers, for to tell a story is to impose form on experience" (1988, p. 87). Jenifer Smith, a contemporary teacher, poet, and researcher, writes movingly of her struggle to find a satisfying way of describing her experience of teaching over a ten-year period in Countesthorpe, England.

Like many of us, she writes not only to communicate with others, but also to discover herself (1991, p. 123). During the course of her graduate studies, Smith felt "dislike of the stridency of many articles about teaching, and the oppressive need to justify . . . contained within a mode of discourse that was reductionist rather than expansive" (1991, p. 122). The style of writing useful for explicating research in the technical rational world of the traditional academy does not accommodate her expressive needs. She feels limited by definitions and liberated by stories, juxtapositions, and nonlinear writing (pp. 123, 117). Like her construct of teaching, her writing is often jagged, deceptively simple, and layered.

Smith's "Setting the Cat among the Pigeons: A Not So Sentimental Journey to the Heart of Teaching" is a moving and insightful pastiche of poetry, academic and personal writing, autobiography, and segments of journals and diaries in which Smith "peers around the corners of [her] own teaching" (1991, p. 116). Just as African-American writers have built on the slave narrative to create works as diverse as Robert Johnson's *Middle Passage* (1990) and Toni Morrison's *Beloved* (1987), so Smith has, with the encouragement and support of her graduate supervisor,

Bill Brookes, extended considerably the confines of the
envelope containing the discourse of reflective practice.
On a recent visit to England, I was priviliged to read the
graduate thesis from which "Setting the Cat" is excerpted.
In the longer work, Smith reveals that it was not easy to
find institutional approval for her writing at first. Clearly
one of the advantages of teaching narratives to teacher-
educators is that they offer aspiring and experienced
teachers alike alternative models for research and writing.
Bill Brookes and the editors of *English Education* recognized that, and we are enormously enriched as a result.
"Setting the Cat" helped me move from teacher-reader to
teacher-researcher and -writer.

Finally, since the teaching narratives are the testimony
of reformers, they are indispensable to teacher-educators
who wish to fortify preservice and developing teachers to
"teach against the grain." This is how Marilyn Cochran-
Smith refers to reform teaching—teaching by educators
who are change agents and so regard their activism as
integral to their work (1991, p. 279). She describes the
complexity of preparing teachers to be reformers by
explaining:

Teaching against the grain stems from, but also generates,
critical perspectives on the macro-level relationships of power,
labor, and ideology—relationships that *are* perhaps best exam-
ined at the university, where sustained and systematic study is
possible. But teaching against the grain is also deeply embedded in the culture and history of teaching at individual schools
and in the biographies of individual teachers and their individual
or collaborative efforts to alter curricula, raise questions about
common practices, and resist inappropriate decisions. These
relationships can only be explored in schools in the company of
experienced teachers who are themselves engaged in complex,
situation-specific, and sometimes losing struggles to work against
the grain. (1991, p. 280)

Cochran-Smith goes on to explain two approaches to

preparing preservice teachers for the work of reform: "critical dissonance" and "collaborative resonance." Critical dissonance emphasizes the incongruity between the critical perspective fostered by university studies and the existing instructional and institutional practices found in schools, particularly during the student teaching experience. Collaborative resonance connects the student's learning at the university with the lived experience in schools through a process of co-labor, which ideally occurs during the student teaching experience. Cochran-Smith clearly favors the latter approach; she describes the results of this fusion of the emic and etic during student teaching experiences in four Philadelphia schools. These experiences paired students with reforming teachers and included regularly scheduled, three-way conversations among the supervising teacher from the university, the cooperating teacher, and the student teacher. One of the conclusions she draws from these carefully structured student teaching situations is that:

Working with experienced school-based reformers exposes student teachers to alternative visions of teaching that enrich but also alter the perspectives they learn in their university courses as well as the perspectives they learn from the larger culture of teaching. . . . One significant way to expand and build on reform efforts is to link student teachers with experienced and new educational reformers. (pp. 306-7)

Unfortunately, as Cochran-Smith acknowledges, the student teaching experiences she details are not typical (p. 304). However, because some who taught against the grain recorded their struggles, it *is* possible for all teacher educators to link preservice and developing teachers with the reformers who wrote teaching narratives so that these crucial three-way conversations can take place. Like the slave narratives they so much resemble, teaching narratives have for too long been neglected, and even scorned. It is my hope that in these pages I have restored them to their rightful place in the curriculum of teacher education.

As I remarked earlier, the Civil War liberated the slaves. But in the thirty years since I began my teaching journey at Smithfield, although many approaches to curriculum and methodology have come and gone, little has happened to improve the lot of the people who are struggling to learn and to teach in the schools. Therefore, it is now more crucial than ever to actively engage aspiring and developing teachers in productive thinking about the nature of their own teaching, and that of the schools. This intellectual and emotional involvement can be fostered through the use of the teaching narratives, which are, in fact, designed to involve their readers and move them to action. Clearly, these provocative autobiographical narratives are a precious legacy from which we still have much to learn.

Bibliography

Applebee, A. N. 1974. *Tradition and Reform in the Teaching of English: A History*. Urbana, Il.: National Council of Teachers of English.

Ashton-Warner, S. 1959. *Spinster*. New York: Simon and Schuster.

———. [1963] 1986. *Teacher*. New York: Simon and Schuster. Reprint.

———. 1972. *Spearpoint*. New York: Knopf.

———. 1979. *I Passed This Way*. New York: Knopf.

Booth, W. C. 1988. *The Company We Keep: An Ethics of Fiction*. Berkeley: University of California Press.

Braithwaite, E. R. 1959. *To Sir, with Love*. London: Bodley.

Brause, R., and Mayher, J. 1991. "Concluding and Beginning." In R. Brause and J. Mayher, eds. *Search and Research: What the Inquiring Teacher Needs to Know*, pp. 207-10. New York: Falmer Press.

Braxton, J. M. 1989. *Black Women Writing Autobiography: A Tradition within a Tradition*. Philadelphia: Temple University Press.

Breines, W. 1992. *Young, White, and Miserable: Growing up Female in the Fifties*. Boston: Beacon Press.

Cisneros, S. 1991. *The House on Mango Street*. New York: Vintage Contemporaries.

Cochran-Smith, M. 1991. "Learning to Teach against the Grain."

Harvard Educational Review, 19(3), 279-310.

Cochran-Smith, M., and Lytle, S. 1990. "Research on Teaching and Teaching Research: The Issues that Divide." *Educational Researcher*, 61, 2-11.

———. 1992. "Teacher Research as a Way of Knowing." *Harvard Educational Review*, 62(4), 447-70.

Coles, R. 1989. "Introduction." In R. Coles, *The Call of Stories: Teaching and the Moral Imagination*, pp. xi-xx. Boston: Houghton Mifflin.

Conroy, P. 1972. *The Water Is Wide*. Boston: Houghton Mifflin.

Cremin, L. A. 1961. *The Transformation of the School: Progressivism in American Education*. New York: Random House.

Cuban, L. 1984. *How Teachers Taught: Constancy and Change in Amercan Classrooms, 1890-1980*. New York: Longman.

Decker, S. 1969. *An Empty Spoon*. New York: Harper and Row.

Duckworth, E. 1987. *"The Having of Wonderful Ideas" and Other Essays on Teaching and Learning*. New York: Teachers College Press.

Eagleton, T. 1983. *Literary Theory: An Introduction*. Minneapolis: University of Minnesota Press.

Edwards, P., ed. 1967. *The Encyclopedia of Philosophy*. New York: Macmillan.

Eggleston, E. [1871] 1957. *The Hoosier School-Master*. New York: Sagamore Press. First published 1871.

Erikson, E. H. 1968. *Identity: Youth and Crisis*. New York: Norton.

Gates, H. L., Jr. 1987. *The Classic Slave Narratives*. New York: Penguin.

Gilyard, K. 1991. *Voices of the Self: A Study of Language Competence*. Detroit: Wayne State University Press.

Gordon, J. W. 1946. *Country School Diary*. New York: Dell Publishing Company.

Grumet, M. R. 1988. *Bitter Milk: Women and Teaching*. Amherst: University of Massachusetts Press.

Hampel, R. L. 1986. *The Last Little Citadel: American High Schools since 1940*. Boston: Houghton Mifflin.

Heilbrun, C. G. 1988. *Writing a Woman's Life*. New York: Ballantine.

Herndon, J. 1968. *The Way It Spozed to Be*. New York: Simon and Schuster.

———. 1971. *How to Survive in Your Native Land*. New York: Simon and Schuster.

Holbrook, D. 1964. *English for the Rejected: Training Literacy in the Lower Streams of the Secondary School*. New York: Cambridge University Press.

———. (1965). *The Secret Places: Essays on Imaginative Work in English Teaching and on the Culture of the Child*. Tuscaloosa: University of Alabama Press.

Holt, J. [1964] 1982. *How Children Fail*. Reprint. New York: Bantam Doubleday Dell.

———. 1967. *How Children Learn*. New York: Pitman.

Hood, L. 1988. *Sylvia! The Biography of Sylvia Ashton-Warner*. New York: Viking Penguin.

Horton, M. 1990. *The Long Haul: An Autobiography*. New York: Doubleday.

Kaufman, B. 1962. "From a Teacher's Wastebasket." *Saturday Review*, November 17, pp. 58-61.

———. 1964. *Up the Down Staircase*. New York: Hearst.

Knowles, J. G. 1992. "Models for Understanding Pre-Service and Beginning Teachers' Biographies: Illustrations from Case Studies." In I. F. Goodson, ed., *Studying Teachers' Lives*, pp. 99-152. New York: Teachers College Press.

Kohl, H. [1967] 1988. *36 Children*. New York: Plume. Reprint.

Lakoff, G., and Johnson, M. 1980. *Metaphors We Live by*. Chicago: University of Chicago Press.

Marshall, S. 1968. *Adventures in Creative Education*. London: Pergamon Press.

Mayher, J. S. 1990. *Uncommon Sense: Theoretical Practice in Language Education*. Portsmouth, N. H.: Heinemann.

McCutcheon, G. 1992. "Facilitating Teacher Personal Theorizing." In W. Ross, J. E. Cornett, and G. McCutcheon, eds., *Teacher Personal Theorizing: Connecting Curriculum Practice, Theory, and Research*, pp. 179-190. Albany: State University of New York Press.

McDonald, J. P. 1992. "Reading for a Profession." In *Teaching: Making Sense of an Uncertain Craft*, pp. 101-23. New York: Teachers College Press.

Middleton, S. 1992. "Developing a Radical Pedagogy: Autobiography of a New Zealand Sociologist of Women's Education." In I. F. Goodson, ed., *Studying Teachers' Lives*, pp. 18-50. New

York: Teachers College Press.

Nehring, J. 1989. *"Why Do We Gotta Do This Stuff, Mr. Nehring?"*: *Notes from a Teacher's Day in School*. New York: Ballantine Books.

Neill, A. S. [1962] 1968. *Summerhill*. Hammondsworth, England: Pelican Books. Reprint.

Noddings, N. 1984. *Caring: A Feminine Approach to Ethics and Moral Eucation*. Berkeley: University of California Press.

————. 1991. "Stories in Dialogue: Caring and Interpersonal Reasoning." In C. Witherell and N. Noddings, eds., *Stories Lives Tell: Narrative and Dialogue in Education*, pp. 157-70. New York: Teachers College Press.

North, S. 1987. "The Practitioners." In *The Making of Knowledge in Composition: Portrait of an Emerging Field*, pp. 21-55. Upper Montclair, N. J.: Boynton Cook.

Pagano, J. A. 1991. "Moral Fictions: The Dilemma of Theory and Practice." In C. Witherell and N. Noddings, eds., *Stories Lives Tell: Narrative and Dialogue in Education*, pp. 193-206. New York: Teachers College Press.

Paley, V. G. 1979. *White Teacher*. Cambridge: Harvard University Press.

————. 1981. *Wally's Stories*. Cambridge: Harvard University Press.

Perkinson, H. J. 1984. *Learning from Our Mistakes: A Reinterpretation of Twentieth Century Educational Theory*. Westport, Conn.: Greenwood Press.

————. 1987. *Two Hundred Years of American Educational Thought*. New York: University Press of America.

————. 1991. *The Imperfect Panacea: American Faith in Education, 1865-1990*. New York: McGraw-Hill.

Prescott, J. 1989. "E. R. Braithwaite." In H. May, and D. A. Straub, eds., *Contemporary Author New Revision Series*, Vol. 25, pp. 40-41. Detroit, Mich.: Gale Research.

[Review of *Up the Down Staircase*]. 1965. *Time Magazine*, February 12, p. 96.

Rose, M. 1989. *Lives on the Boundary: The Struggles and Achievements of America's Underprepared*. New York: Free Press.

Rosenblatt, L. 1983. *Literature as Exploration*. New York: Modern Language Association.

Ross, W. 1992. "Teacher Personal Theorizing and Reflective

Practice in Teacher Education." In W. Ross, J. E. Cornett, and G. McCutcheon, eds., *Teacher Personal Theorizing: Connecting Curriculum Practice, Theory, and Research*, pp. 179-90. Albany: State University of New York Press.

Rowe, D. 1988. *The Successful Self*. London: Fontana.

Ryan, K., ed. 1970. *Don't Smile until Christmas: Accounts of the First Year of Teaching*. Chicago: University of Chicago Press.

Salmon, P. 1988. *Psychology for Teachers: An Alternative Approach*. London: Hutchinson.

Schön, D. A. 1983. *The Reflective Practitioner: How Professionals Think in Action*. New York: Basic Books.

Schubert, W. T. 1991. "Teacher Lore: A Basis for Understanding Praxis." In C. Witherell and N. Noddings, eds., *Stories Lives Tell: Narrative and Dialogue in Education*, pp. 207-33. New York: Teachers College Press.

Sikes, P. 1985. "The Life Cycle of the Teacher." In S. J. Ball and I. F. Goodson, eds., *Teachers' Lives and Careers*, pp. 27-60. Philadelphia: Falmer Press.

Smith, J. 1991. "Setting the Cat among the Pigeons: A Not So Sentimental Journey to the Heart of Teaching." *English Education* [Special issue on reflective practice], *23*, 68-126.

Stuart, J. 1973. *To Teach, to Love: What Teaching Means to a Famous American Teacher-Writer*. Baltimore, Md.: Penguin.

Tannen, D. 1992. *You Just Don't Understand: Women and Men in Conversation*. New York: Ballantine Books.

Taylor, K. 1963. "The How Is Mightier Than the What". *The New York Times Book Review*, September 8, pp. 1, 36.

Van Til, W. 1983. *My Way of Looking at It: An Autobiography*. Terre Haute, Ind.: Lake Lure Press.

Walkerdine, V. 1981. "Sex, Power, and Pedagogy." *Screen Education*, 38, 14-24.

Warriner, J. E. 1958. *English Grammar and Composition: Complete Course*, Vol. 6. New York: Harcourt Brace.

Welker, R. 1992. *The Teacher as Expert: A Theoretical and Historical Examination*. Albany: State University of New York Press.

Index

Fictionalized names of real people appear in their entirety; authors are indexed by surname and initial(s).

About the Author

JANE ISENBERG, Associate Professor of English at Hudson County Community College in New Jersey with a Ph.D. in applied linguistics from New York University, has over thirty years of experience in the urban classroom. She began her career teaching high school English in 1962 immediately after graduating from Vassar College.